CLEVER BABY

CLEVER BABY

100 PLAY IDEAS TO BOOST YOUR CHILD'S DEVELOPMENT

SIMONE CAVE AND DR CAROLINE FERTLEMAN

METRO BOOKS
NEW YORK

We dedicate this book to Mike and Judy Cave,
and Rosemary and Leonard Fertleman.

Text copyright © Simone Cave and Caroline Fertleman 2011
Specially commissioned photography © Emma Peios 2011

Metro Books
122 Fifth Avenue
New York, NY 10011

ISBN 978-1-4351-3000-5

Printed and bound in China

10 9 8 7 6 5 4 3 2 1

Disclaimer

The author, packager and publisher cannot accept responsibility
for any injury or damage resulting from the use, or misuse, of
the suggestions made in this book. The information contained
is intended as a general guide and should not be relied upon for
medical, health or other professional advice. Please consult a medical
professional if you are in any doubt about your child's health.

Contents

Introduction 6

Part One

New Baby
Birth to Six Months 9

Part Two

Older Baby
Six to Twelve Months 59

Part Three

Toddler
Twelve to Twenty-four Months 109

Development Time Line 200 • Resources 204 • Index 205
About the Authors 207 • Acknowledgements 208

Introduction

Playing with your baby is essential if she is to become a happy, creative and intelligent individual. Research shows that regularly enjoying a few simple activities together will help everything from her fine motor skills and her ability to stand and walk, to brain development and speech, as well as how she interacts and socializes with others. Of course, it's difficult to find time to play with your baby and it's easy to feel guilty, but you're not alone – no parent *ever* thinks they spend enough time playing with their little one.

However, we hope that understanding the importance of play will motivate you to play with your child more often. When you know how certain activities help your baby's brain to develop or, perhaps, strengthen particular muscles which will eventually help her to walk, the effort of hanging up a mobile or getting out the playdough seems all the more worthwhile.

In this book we've included plenty of activities that take just a few minutes and yet have profound benefits for your baby's development. We know from experience (we're both mothers of three) that there will be days when you're exhausted and simply won't be able to face an elaborate play session, and that's fine. In fact, a few minutes of play here and there each day is better than a marathon play session once a week. Even as your child approaches her second birthday, fifteen minutes is about the maximum that she'll want to spend on a single activity.

It isn't necessary to be glued to your baby or to supervise her every waking minute. You'll probably find that if you spend time on an activity with her, she may sometimes continue the activity by herself – and she'll still be learning. But watch out if she seems exceptionally good at playing alone as this can occasionally indicate a hearing problem.

The book is divided into three sections categorized by age to correspond with your baby's development: birth to six months; six to twelve months; and twelve to twenty-four months. Within each section we've ordered the activities roughly by age. But, of course, all babies develop at different rates, so feel free to jump ahead or, if your child loves a certain activity, let her play this for as long as she wants to even if she's moved onto the next section. There are no rules; if she's having fun she'll almost certainly be learning.

With regards to gender, we alternate between 'she' and 'he' from one activity to the next, depending on the sex of the baby shown in the photographs. This is simply to ensure the references to girls and boys is as even as possible. All the activities are suitable for children of both sexes.

Please don't feel that you should go through the book ticking off every activity as you try it. This would soon make playing with your baby seem like a chore. Everyone is different, so if you can't cook don't feel obliged to start making bread. Likewise, if arts and crafts aren't your thing, there's no need to rush off to a craft-supply shop. You won't be the only person in your baby's life; she may have lots of enthusiastic grandparents and family friends who will each have their specialities and abilities. So let the 'cook' among you do the baking with your child and the 'artist' can do the crafts.

Our advice is that you simply choose the activities that appeal to you personally. If you're enjoying yourself, you'll feel more relaxed, enthusiastic and patient when you're playing with your baby, and that's definitely a good thing. That way, both you and your child will love the time you spend together.

Simone Cave and Caroline Fertleman

Part One

New Baby
Birth to Six Months

As you gaze in wonder at your newborn baby, you'll find yourself fascinated by his every movement and gurgle, and over the coming weeks you'll be continually amazed by his incredible capacity for learning. Playing with your baby in a stimulating and fun way will make a vast difference to his development. So read on to discover how to keep him amused and entertained during the next few months.

Lots of new moms struggle to find time to go to the toilet, have a shower or clean their teeth. If this sounds like you, the thought of fitting in playtime as well may send you into a bit of a spin. One of the main obstacles to playing in the early days is that your baby sleeps so often. And when he's awake you're busy feeding him, winding him and changing his nappy. This leaves little time for play. But you'll find that over the following weeks and months your baby is gradually awake and alert for longer, which will give you more opportunity for play. In the meantime, please don't put pressure on yourself; playing with a very young baby for as little as a minute at a time is sufficient to give him enjoyment and boost his development.

From day one

You can play with your baby from the moment he's born, by making faces at him or putting your finger or some soft fabric in his palm to stimulate his sense of touch. He'll automatically grip because of his newborn reflex response. In the early weeks you'll find that the best time to play with your baby is after a feed and a nap, when he's not feeling hungry or tired. During a nappy change is another opportunity for play, as long as he seems happy. If he's fractious, simply concentrate on a quick change and give him a cuddle as soon as you can. Likewise, bath time can present a good opportunity for play, particularly after about six weeks when most babies start to really enjoy having a bath. And, if you've got a rear-facing pram or buggy, you can make faces and sounds and 'chat' to your baby when you're out and about. When your baby is very young, you can try to snatch any opportunity when he's awake to play with him for a few minutes. It doesn't have to be anything too formal; just pulling silly faces while you wait in a queue at the shops will be stimulating and beneficial for your baby. We've included a wide range of easy activities; try out the ones that suit you best and build play into you and your baby's daily routine.

Does he like it?

In just a few weeks your baby will be able to indicate when he's particularly enjoying an activity by widening his eyes and kicking his legs. And from six weeks he'll start to smile – when he looks you in the eye and grins, you will be in no doubt whatsoever that he's enjoying playing with you, so do continue. But if he turns his head away or avoids eye contact, it's a sign that he's tired and has had enough. Other signs that your baby wants to stop include grizzling, yawning, pulling his ears or generally seeming less energetic. Do stop playing with your baby as soon as you spot these signs because he's giving you a very clear message that he's tired. If he sticks his lip out or his mouth quivers, it probably means that he's feeling frightened and is about to cry, so again it's time to stop playing. You can use the happy ☺ and sad ☹ faces to record your baby's reaction to each activity.

Enjoy every minute

The first six months of your baby's life is a staggering time for developmental leaps. You'll witness your tiny newborn change into a smiling, bouncing baby who can grab at toys, kick with vigour and even shake a rattle. Babies are able to make sense of the world long before they can talk, and they absorb so much as they start to understand what they see and hear. So this is a great opportunity to boost your baby's potential and to try to maximize his brain development so that he really does become a very clever little baby.

1 Pulling Faces

Babies can imitate facial expressions at birth, so you can have fun staring at your baby and making faces straightaway. Hold her about 20–25 cm (8–10 in) away, the optimal distance for her to focus, then spend a minute or two sticking out your tongue and opening and closing your mouth. Her vision will be quite blurred so do these actions slowly, make them very exaggerated and give her plenty of time to respond. Babies love faces, so she'll be fascinated and, if she doesn't fall asleep or get hungry, she may try to mimic you. After a day or so your baby will lose this biological reflex, so her capacity to mimic your facial expressions will disappear, but the skill

What you need

- An expressive face

will return at about two months. By six months she'll be very good at it so, as well as smiling, you can try showing your teeth, blinking and blowing raspberries. You can even make noises such as 'buzz' and 'aaah', and expressive noises like 'boo', 'maa' and 'pah' that will make your mouth interesting to watch. Your baby won't be able to copy the noises at first, but she will be very curious and will watch you closely. Babies love to look at lights and black-and-white contrasting tones, so don't wear a black-and-white top or sit near a bright light when you're doing this as it will distract her.

At around six weeks your baby will start to smile when she sees you. Spend time smiling at her and watch as she responds by smiling back at you. The social smile is a little fleeting at first but after a couple of weeks your baby will start grinning at everyone.

Benefits

Bonding
Making faces is a wonderful way to bond with your newborn and it is quite a magical moment when your tiny infant gently responds to your expression. This is particularly beneficial for the relationship between father and child because dads obviously can't bond by breastfeeding.

Vision
Newborn babies have very blurred vision and will only see large shapes and shadows, so you will have to make your expressions large and slow: for example, opening and closing your mouth very wide and very slowly. But, even at birth, your baby's eye muscles will be developing and every tiny movement she makes as she looks at you will help her muscles to strengthen.

Focusing
After two months, your baby's vision will be clearer and she will start to fix on or stare at your face. Focusing on your face will enable your baby to practise controlling her eye muscles.

Communication
As your baby watches your face and copies your expressions she is learning social interaction and developing her sensitivity to social cues. The more she stares at people's faces, the more observant she will be of their changing expressions. This is actually a very early stage in language development and your baby will go on to watch your lips closely when you talk and this will help her to learn language. Eventually, she will closely watch facial expressions and mannerisms when communicating with others.

2 What's that Sound?

At birth your baby will be able to hear well, although not perfectly, but after just a month his hearing will be fully developed. He will particularly like high-pitched sounds, and you'll probably find yourself talking to him in a higher voice than you would normally use. He'll love to hear you talking and you'll see him paying close attention when he hears a voice that he knows. Babies particularly love soft vocalization and cooing.

Your baby will also enjoy listening to other gentle, high-pitched sounds, such as wind chimes and music boxes, that stand out from the background hum of life. Take the time to wind up a music box for your baby to listen to, and perhaps hang some wind chimes by a window and position him nearby in his Moses basket. The high-pitched sound of bird song is also popular with babies so, if you've got a garden, put him outside in the shade on a warm day to listen to the birds singing. He may also stop and listen to a phone ringing, the bell on a cat's collar or the beeping of a cooker timer – anything that has a distinct, high sound that he only hears intermittently.

What you need

Any of the following:

- Your voice
- Music box
- Wind chimes
- Keys to rattle

NEW BABY

Don't be afraid to expose your baby to everyday sounds such as the television, radio, vacuum cleaner, loud voices or sirens from passing emergency vehicles. None of these will damage his ears at normal volumes, although he may be startled by loud, unfamiliar noises – even clapping may make him cry until he is three months old. The upside to this is that it gives you a sign that his hearing is good, but he may need some big cuddles if he gets very upset.

Although the occasional loud sound that lasts just a second or two won't do any harm, persistent loud noise could damage your baby's hearing. It's particularly important to avoid playing music too loudly – not only can it damage hearing, it's not very soothing for babies. Of course, it's fine to play music when your baby is around, but if you have to raise your voice to talk, it's too loud.

Benefits

Soothes and relaxes

Mothers have always sung to their babies as it has a very calming effect. Babies become familiar with their mother's voice in the womb, so this is a very comforting sound. Likewise, if you always play a music box before a sleep, your baby will find its familiar tune soothing.

Helps baby get used to noise

Babies are quite sensitive to noise and it doesn't take much to make them jump. Exposing your baby to noises will make them more familiar and acceptable to him.

Boosts memory

If your baby hears the same tune enough times, he will start to remember it. You could try playing a tune at the same time each day, for example just before your baby's bath, so that he learns that the tune means it's bath time. He'll be capable of anticipation as he approaches six months.

Helps locate sounds

At around three months your baby will face you when he hears your voice. Between four and six months he'll easily be able to locate sounds. Shake keys or snap your fingers at either side of his head to see if he turns towards the sound.

3 Something to Watch

Your baby won't always be asleep when she's in her Moses basket and may happily lie awake for a few minutes if there is something to hold her attention. Find a window in your home that you can safely put the basket near. It's fine to put it on the floor, but never use a window ledge, no matter how wide it is.

When babies are born, the eyes' retina cells aren't fully developed, so colours look muted. In the first few weeks your baby won't be able to take in a detailed view but she will be able to see light and dark. Her attention will also be captured by movement, lights and reflections from the window. You could put her where she can watch the trees moving in the breeze, or put her outside under a tree if it's warm enough, or near an open window with a fluttering curtain.

Hang something at a window, perhaps a small teddy bear. Your baby will easily see the light and dark

Safety first

Always keep a close eye on your baby when she's outside.

What you need

- Moses basket

One of the following:

- Interesting window
- Small teddy bear and a ribbon
- Glass prism
- Bird feeder
- Fish tank

contrast of the bear against the window. Tie a ribbon around the bear's neck and attach the other end to a curtain rail or window fitting. On another day you could hang up a different soft toy to see if she notices.

On sunny days a glass prism hung at the window will cast little dancing rainbows around the room that your baby will love to watch. You could try hanging a bird feeder outside a window. Fish tanks also make good viewing for babies. If you have a tank, make a point of putting your baby where she can see it. She will be fascinated by the lights and reflections as well as the moving fish and bubbles.

Do ensure that your baby can actually see all these interesting things from her Moses basket – lie down to check, making sure you allow for the side of the basket. For a better view, you could lie your baby on a play mat or a bath towel folded in half.

Your baby may not want to lie and look at prisms or fluttering curtains for longer than a few minutes; you may notice that she's happy to watch for longer on some days than others. In the early weeks, just a little visual stimulation will be very beneficial. Your baby may show preferences in what she likes to look at – the giveaway is a very intense gaze. Be aware that babies change very quickly in the early weeks and she may soon become fascinated by something else.

Benefits

Reduces flattened head syndrome

A baby's soft skull can become flattened as a result of lying on her back for a long time; this is more common now that parents are advised to put babies down to sleep on their backs. Although completely harmless, parents may worry that their baby has a slightly wonky-shaped head. If your baby always sleeps with her head to the right, this side of her head may become a little flat. Arrange her Moses basket so that she turns her head the other way. This will help to even things out. Activity 5, Tummy Play, is also very beneficial.

Strengthens eye muscles

Watching birds, moving leaves, fluttering curtains or prisms of light will help to strengthen your baby's eye muscles as she focuses.

Strengthens neck muscles

Every time your baby moves her head to look at something, even if it's just a fraction, she will use her neck muscles, so they will gradually get stronger. Again, tummy play is also very helpful in this respect.

4 Let's Talk

Babies can hear the outside world from inside the womb, so they are familiar with the sound of their parents' voices from the moment they are born and they love hearing them. Lots of parents talk to their babies automatically, but if this is your first child and you haven't had much contact with babies previously, you may feel very self-conscious, particularly in the early days when he doesn't respond much. However, talking to your baby is so beneficial that it's a habit well worth getting into. It really doesn't matter what you talk about. Try giving a running commentary as you go about your day: for example, 'Let's have a clean nappy, and put a bit of cream on. That's better.' And so on.

What you need

- Your voice
- Phone

One way to get around the problem of feeling self-conscious is to look at your baby when you're talking on the phone – he'll think you're talking to him and will love it (although don't spend too much time on the phone because it's important to read your baby's cues – this is crucial to communicating with your baby – and it's difficult to observe him closely if you're deep in conversation).

Benefits

Soothes
Because your voice is so familiar to your baby, hearing you talk will have a very soothing and calming effect.

Voice recognition
By regularly hearing familiar voices, your baby will learn to recognize people from their voice alone. So, before too long, when he hears you or anyone else he spends a lot of time with, he'll know who it is.

Language development
Babies listen closely to people talking long before they can understand the words, so hearing you speak is fundamental to your baby learning to talk. Mimicry is very important to language development and it is known that from around nine months some babies can imitate sounds. However, mimicry starts far earlier than this, with some research suggesting that it actually begins in the womb. In one study, researchers observed that French newborn babies cry with a French accent, with a rising melody, which indicates that babies pick up the intonation of language in the womb.

Social interaction and bonding
Chatting to your baby will encourage you to make eye contact as you explain to him what's happening: 'Now, let's lower you gently into the bath; it's nice and warm; there we are, now let's wash your face …' and so on. The more you talk to your baby, the more you will look at his face and observe him trying to communicate with you. You'll notice a quivering lip if he's frightened, or a bright red face if he's got wind. Talking to your baby will make a big difference to how you interact with him as you will respond to the messages he gives you. If you don't chat to your baby when you bath him, for instance, you'll probably find that you drift off into your own thoughtful world, unaware of any tiny clues that your little one is giving out about how he feels and what he needs, and you would probably find that after a while your relationship becomes more mechanical than playful.

5 Tummy Play

From around two weeks you can put your baby on her front to play. She may lift her head briefly – good for muscle development – and you can encourage this by putting brightly coloured toys in front of her. Cuddly toys work well because they have faces. At first she will only be happy on her tummy for a few minutes at a time, but do persevere as after six weeks she'll probably refuse to go on her tummy at all if she's not used to it.

To keep tummy time interesting, experiment with different toys. You could also try a mirror, pictures of faces or a chess board – babies love symmetrical patterns as they appear to swim before their eyes. Better still, get down on the floor with her so that she can see your face – her favourite toy of all.

To give your baby a different view of the world, you could try a baby blow-up ring. Put your baby in the middle and lie her, tummy down, on the side of the ring. Her head will be propped up a little and she'll be able to look around the room.

By eight weeks your baby may be able to reach out and bash nearby toys. Choose toys that rattle or rustle – a scrunched-up ball of newspaper can work. By ten weeks she may be able to lift her head for about ten seconds at a time.

What you need

- Soft mat for your baby to lie on, (or a brightly coloured baby mat, a rug, soft carpet or duvet)
- Blow-up baby ring
- Cuddly toys
- Chess board
- Mirror
- Pictures of faces

ℬenefits

Strengthens neck, trunk and upper back muscles

Tummy play has more strengthening benefits than being on her back.

Strengthens abdominal, back and shoulder muscles

From three months your baby may be able to push her chest off the floor to have a quick look around before collapsing. So put her on her tummy when there's lots going on in the room – perhaps when you have visitors. This will motivate her to pull herself up. You can also continue to put toys in front of your baby so that she can push up and look at them.

Reduces flattened head syndrome

Although harmless, flattened head syndrome is much more common now that babies routinely sleep on their backs because the soft skull can become flattened. Encouraging your baby to play on her front helps to minimize further misshaping of your baby's head.

Relieves wind and colic

Putting your baby on her front can be soothing because the pressure on the tummy seems to relax the gut muscles and relieve wind. Plenty of moms have noticed that tummy time can reduce the severity of colic in the evenings. Don't put your baby on her tummy during a painful attack of wind or colic, though, as she'll want to be cuddled. For more information on colic, see page 43.

Back to sleep

Because babies are now put to sleep on their backs to reduce cot death, they tend to have delayed motor-skill development, so they roll over and crawl later than in the past. This isn't a problem and your baby will catch up in the end, but put her on her front as often as possible to counterbalance the hours she spends asleep on her back. Do make sure she doesn't fall asleep on her front – the safest sleeping position is on her back.

6 Watching You

From just a few weeks of age your baby will love to watch you. Put her in a baby chair; a bouncy chair is ideal because, not only will she be sitting fairly upright, she will be able to wriggle around and use her muscles. Car seats are not suitable for this purpose as they are very rigid and restrict movement. Let her watch you go about your daily activities. It doesn't matter what you're doing; she will be quite happy sitting in the bedroom while you fold the laundry! Stop and say 'hello' from time to time so that she can enjoy the social interaction. Remember that in the early weeks your baby will only be able to see strong contrasts, so try to stand by a window as much as possible so that she can see your outline clearly. From the second month she will be aware of you coming and going, so say 'hello' and 'goodbye' as you enter and leave the room.

You could also put your baby in the kitchen while you cook. Just ensure that her chair is well away from anything that could spill or be dropped on her. And, if you can fit the baby chair in the bathroom, she

Safety first

Never leave your baby unattended in a bouncy chair.
Only ever put a bouncy chair on the floor.

What you need

- Baby chair

could watch while you have a shower. Of course, there's no need to stick to your baby like glue all the time; just do this if she's grizzly and you happen to want a shower. It's also important that you can leave your baby's sight without her becoming upset.

Many babies love the hustle and bustle of busy family life so, if you have other children and there's lots of coming and going, she'll love watching and listening to everything that's going on.

You will probably find that, after about three months, your baby is happy to sit in her chair for longer periods of time as her vision improves and she is able to stay awake for longer. However, from about six or seven months, when she starts to get mobile, the chair may seem like a prison and she will want to escape and get moving.

Helps develop the eye muscles
Your baby's eye muscles will strengthen as she focuses on you and watches what you're doing.

Boosts understanding of the world
Your baby will be seeing things for the very first time: if you drop something, she'll see it fall to the floor – the first step in learning about gravity; when you chop vegetables, she will observe how the knife makes a noise when it moves up and down. As well as developing an understanding of cause and effect, she will also get used to various noises.

Eases reflux
Some babies are particularly sensitive to reflux (acidic regurgitation and heartburn after feeding). If your baby is troubled by this condition, sitting in a more upright position can help to ease the problem.

Relieves cold symptoms
Newborn babies can become particularly blocked up if they catch a cold as they spend so much time on their backs. Being upright helps any excess mucus to drain out of the nasal passages.

7 Entertain Me

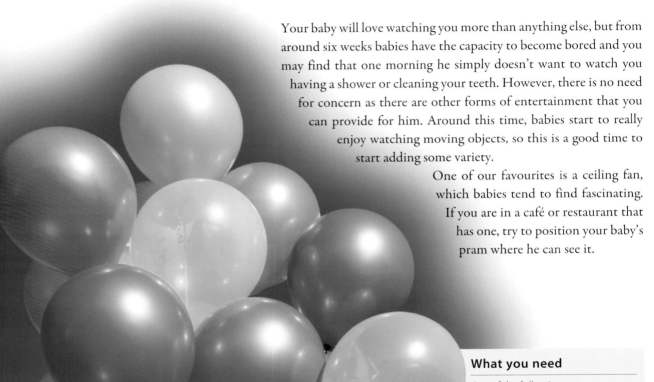

Your baby will love watching you more than anything else, but from around six weeks babies have the capacity to become bored and you may find that one morning he simply doesn't want to watch you having a shower or cleaning your teeth. However, there is no need for concern as there are other forms of entertainment that you can provide for him. Around this time, babies start to really enjoy watching moving objects, so this is a good time to start adding some variety.

One of our favourites is a ceiling fan, which babies tend to find fascinating. If you are in a café or restaurant that has one, try to position your baby's pram where he can see it.

What you need

Any of the following:

- Ceiling fan
- Floor fan (with a fan guard)
- Bamboo stick
- Ribbons in strong colours
- Balloons in strong colours
- String
- Torch

You could also set up a fan on the floor and place a stick tied with ribbons or balloons beside it so that they blow in the breeze – or tie the items to the fan guard itself if the design of the fan allows. Choose bright, strong colours as your baby will find these easier to see than pastel shades. Place your baby in his bouncy chair so that he can watch this spectacle, taking care to position him so that he can't reach out and touch the fan or anything hanging from it.

In the evenings, try putting a light behind the ribbons or balloons so that they form shadows on the wall for your baby to enjoy. The contrast will be easy for him to see, and babies do love to look at lights.

There are a number of other variations you could try, such as flicking a torch around a darkened room, or making shadows on the walls with your hands: for example, a flying bird or a dog. Look at what you have around the house and get creative.

Benefits

Has a calming effect

After the initial thrill of watching the ceiling fan, the rhythmic whirring will soothe your baby and the background or 'white' noise may even send him to sleep. However, don't let him become dependent on watching a fan in order to get to sleep.

Provides stimulation

Having something interesting to watch will stimulate your baby and prevent boredom. Babies can get a bit fractious if they're bored; this peaks at around three months and usually improves once they start to become mobile at around four months when they roll.

Improves vision

Focusing on something interesting will enable your baby to practise controlling his eye muscles. Watching a moving object will help him to develop his tracking skills; as his brain matures he will be able to anticipate an object's movement and follow it with his eyes.

8 Mobile Fun

A mobile hanging above your baby's cot or changing table will give him something to look at, particularly if it moves in the breeze. When choosing a mobile, there are a few things to think about. Firstly, as newborn babies find it easier to see black-and-white objects than coloured ones, you could set up a black-and-white mobile above his cot to entertain him in the early weeks. From about six weeks he'll start to see bright colours and find these more stimulating than black-and-white, so you may then wish to change the hanging toys. You may like to have a go at making your own mobile (*see opposite*). A major advantage of doing this is that you can easily adapt it to suit your baby's rapid development in the early weeks. It is best to avoid pastel colours as these will be difficult for your baby to see. Babies do like anything that reflects light, so small mirrors or shiny objects are a good choice. If you don't mind spending a little more money, you could get a mobile that plays tunes and rotates as these are very popular with babies.

Hang the mobile about 25 cm (10 in) from your baby's face so that he can focus on it comfortably without being able to reach out and grab it.

What you need

- Mobile

Safety first

It's important to ensure that all objects are firmly attached to avoid any danger of them dropping onto your baby.

Once your baby can sit up, and then stand, you'll need to move the mobile to a much higher position to ensure that he can't grab hold of it.

Benefits

Boosts brain development

Babies need stimulation, and having things to look at helps to strengthen the neural circuits in the area of the brain that controls thought. Also, when your baby moves his head to watch his mobile, he'll not only strengthen his neck muscles but will also send messages from the motor areas of the brain to the nerves that move those muscles.

Strengthens eye muscles

If the mobile moves, your baby will try to move his eyes to keep it in his field of vision. This will strengthen his eye muscles and help him learn to move both eyes together and adjust his head at the same time.

How to make a mobile

The easiest way to make a mobile is to take several pieces of string of different lengths and tie a variety of objects from the ends, then hang each length of string from the ceiling. Begin with symmetrical black-and-white patterns painted on card cut into circles, diamonds and squares, and mirrors – or card covered with tinfoil (although they're not particularly pretty, your baby will love them). Then you could progress to brightly coloured objects such as small soft toys or cardboard cutouts of faces.

9 Who's Ringing?

Attaching bells to your baby's bouncy chair will allow her to make the bells ring when she moves. This will not only encourage her to wriggle about, but to listen too. You should be able to find small bells in craft shops, pet shops, supermarkets or online. The kind that attaches to cat collars is ideal, but any lightweight bells will work. Tie the bells around your baby's chair. Cut off any excess string so that your baby can't get caught up in it.

What you need

- About six small bells
- String or ribbon

Benefits

Develops understanding of cause and effect
As your baby moves and hears the bells, she will gradually learn that it is her movement that controls the sound.

Encourages movement
The realization that she makes the bells ring by moving will encourage your baby to move more. Even tiny movements will build muscle and develop motor skills.

10 Wear your Baby

Try using a baby carrier at home as well as when you go out. This way you'll be able to carry on with your chores and your baby will be soothed as you carry her. She'll need to face you until she is three months old, then she can start facing outwards to get a really good view of the world.

What you need

- Baby carrier

Benefits

Develops head control
Being in a baby carrier requires more back- and neck-muscle strength than lying down.

Reduces crying
Research shows that carrying a baby reduces crying. Being close to and smelling mom will calm your baby, and the movement will remind her of her days in the womb. This can be particularly beneficial for colicky babies who can get very fractious. If she still won't stop crying, try a bit of dancing and gentle spinning.

Bonding
As your baby cries less, you'll relax and enjoy her company and will be more likely to chatter to her and have fun – perhaps looking in the mirror together.

11 Touchy Feely

Babies are born with a good sense of touch, so make the most of this by collecting together a selection of different fabrics such as satin, velvet, cotton, wool, fake fur and leather. Gently run them through your baby's hands, or help him to grip them, and perhaps stroke them over his cheeks. As your baby gets older, he'll be able to reach and eventually grab at the fabric himself and will start to put them in his mouth; babies' mouths are very sensitive and this is a good way for them to explore new things.

You should be able to find different fabrics from haberdashery shops – ask for any off-cuts because you don't need very big pieces. Even swatches from sofa and carpet shops can work well – try to include lots of bright colours as your baby will enjoy these. Put your collection into a bag (not plastic) and give it to your baby to play with from time to time.

What you need

Any of the following:

- A range of textures
- Baby-touch books
- Clothes made from a variety of fabrics

Benefits

Encourages discovery of the world

A section of the brain called the parietal lobe controls touch, taste and your baby's ability to recognize objects. Your baby won't be ready to try different tastes until he is weaned (usually six months), but giving him different textures to touch is a good way to stimulate development in this part of the brain now.

Increases sensitivity

Although babies are born with a good sense of touch, they are unable to interpret what they touch. By playing with fabrics, your baby will learn to make sense of the different textures and objects he touches and will discover the difference between hard, soft, smooth, rough and so on.

Hand–eye coordination

Grabbing at different fabrics and reaching out to his textured books will improve your baby's hand–eye coordination. It requires considerable skill to judge the distance he has to reach, and then accurately grab at whatever he's aiming for.

Alternatively, you could give your baby a furry soft toy to touch or a board book with textured illustrations. The latter are widely available from book shops and libraries; your baby will love looking at such books with you, and you can help him to touch the textured areas on each page.

Make a point of wearing different fabrics; from birth, babies will often grip your clothes when they are being fed or carried. However, don't wear anything that is difficult to clean – it would be awful to end up resenting your baby because he's been sick on your best leather coat or a dry-clean-only silk dress!

When your baby becomes a toddler, you could use the fabrics to help with language development: teach him to describe the different textures and colours, or name the materials.

12 Bath Together

Bathing with your baby is a wonderful experience and you can do this from birth. If you use a bath mat to prevent slipping, it's possible to step into the bath while holding your baby, although it may be easier if your partner passes her to you. Lie your baby on your chest and enjoy the skin-to-skin contact while you gently swoosh water over her.

As your baby gets older you can encourage her to splash with her hands and kick with her legs. Use a plastic cup to pour water over her tummy and legs. From about four months she'll delight

What you need

- Bath mat
- Bath robe
- Plastic cup

in splashing water in your face and making you do a pretend cough and splutter. It is fine to splash your baby; young babies don't mind getting water in their face too much and it's good to get them used to it. You could play a game by warning your baby that you're going to splash her – say, 'ready, steady, splash' – then gently slosh some water over her face. If she gets upset, stop and wipe the water off her face – you don't want to make her anxious about water.

Babies often wee in the bath, but there is no need to worry about this because urine is sterile. Thankfully, it's quite rare for babies to poo in the bath.

You will need to have the bath water cooler than you would normally, and when you get out of the bath you will need to put on a bath robe because, unless your partner is available to help, you won't have time to get yourself dry until you have dried and dressed your baby.

Benefits

Bonding

Bathing with your baby is deeply comforting – she has your undivided attention because you're relaxing in the bath and not thinking about getting chores done. Skin-to-skin contact is said to calm babies and reduce crying. Lots of dads enjoy bathing with their babies too; this is a fun way for them to spend time together in the early weeks.

Builds water confidence

If your baby is with you in the bath, she should feel safe and not worry too much if she gets splashed. If she is happy to have water on her face, you'll avoid the usual hair-washing battles when she's a toddler. It will also be useful for when she learns to swim because she'll be more confident about putting her head in the water. Splashing in the bath is where dad really comes into his own because he will probably be less careful than mom, and boisterous water games will do wonders for your baby's water confidence.

Aids muscle development

When your baby is on your tummy, she'll be lying on her front, which is especially good for muscle development. Kicking and splashing in the water will also help. Your baby is likely to move around more in the water than she would normally as she will enjoy the sensation of the water flowing over her skin. This will also help her sensory development.

13 Leg Exercises

When your baby is on the changing mat without his trousers or a nappy on, spend a minute or two 'cycling' his legs, gently holding his ankles or feet. You can also do 'scissor legs' with his outstretched legs. The advantage of playing this game when your baby isn't wearing a nappy is that he'll be less bundled up in clothes so his legs will move freely and there will be no restrictions, but you can do it when he has a nappy on too.

One variation is to play with your baby's arms, winding his hands around each other, first in one direction and then the other. This is a good game to try in the mornings when you are lying in bed: prop your knees up to make a back rest for your baby and have fun with his hands. Then, if possible, pass your baby to your partner so that he can continue the game while you get dressed or have a quick doze.

What you need

- Clean nappy
- Changing mat

As you play these games you can add even more fun by singing to your baby. Either sing some songs that you know or make some up, or chant some rhymes. From about four months, babies really appreciate singing with their parents.

Benefits

Aids muscle development

Even slight movements will help your baby's muscle development, and peddling his legs will help to strengthen his abdominal muscles and improve his gross motor skills. It will also familiarize him with moving his legs alternately. Winding your baby's hands will help to strengthen his shoulder- and arm muscles. As your baby experiences the sensation of his arms winding first in one direction and then another, it will stimulate motor development, eventually helping coordination.

Promotes interaction

Whether you are scissoring your baby's legs or winding his hands, you'll almost certainly be watching his face. These games are good for interaction as you will have to maintain eye contact with your baby to ensure that he is still happy and enjoying the game. Hopefully he'll be loving it and smiling. If he doesn't seem so happy then stop – you can always try another day.

Eases nappy rash

Nappy rash is caused by urine being broken down by bacteria in the stools and forming ammonia, which burns the skin, making it red and sore. If your baby suffers from this, 'nappy off' time will certainly help, so put his changing mat on the floor, place an old clean towel underneath his bottom in case of any accidents, then have fun playing. As little as five minutes without a nappy on will help your baby's nappy rash, and two hours will make a dramatic difference.

Boosts memory

Older babies and toddlers are more likely to remember the words to songs if they have learnt actions, so repeating a song or rhyme as you do the movements with your baby will stimulate his memory. As your baby approaches six months he will have the developmental capability to anticipate, and he may expect you to wind his hands or cycle his legs whenever he hears a particular song.

14 Baby Gym

From two months, babies are able to grasp at objects purposefully and will start to reach out and bash at things, so this is a good age to start popping your baby under a baby gym for a few minutes from time to time, and also to put a string of beads or toys across her cot or pram. By three months your baby will be reasonably skilled at hitting her targets.

Brightly coloured plastic baby gyms that make a noise are always a big hit with babies. These are readily available from toy shops and baby shops and can often be bought second-hand – if you do get one that's already

What you need

Any of the following:

- Baby gym
- Helium balloon
- Elastic
- Plastic toys
- String of beads

been used, do make sure you clean it thoroughly before you let your baby play with it.

Also popular are play mats with play arches over the top, which have fabric toys dangling down for babies to reach. These are certainly prettiest to have in your home but probably not as popular with babies who are drawn to gaudiness and noise. If you choose this option, go for a brightly coloured one rather than pastel shades because it will be easier for your baby to see. You can also buy mini-gym arches that fit over a baby chair, although do bear in mind that it's important for your baby to spend time lying flat on the floor or playing in her cot; being in a baby chair can restrict movement.

If you don't have a baby gym, it's easy to improvise. Simply dangle a toy above your baby and let her try to grab it, making sure you give her lots of praise when she does. You can also let your baby play with a helium balloon. Choose a shiny one that reflects light and put the string in your baby's hand; she'll enjoy tugging the string and watching the balloon move. Of course, don't leave her alone with the string for safety reasons.

You could even make your own baby gym. Tie brightly coloured, smooth plastic toys, such as rattles, to a piece of elastic and fix this across the cot. Make sure the height allows your baby to hit the toys with her hands but isn't low enough for her to grab the elastic itself.

Benefits

Improves hand–eye coordination

At first your baby will move her arms quite jerkily but, as she practises bashing the toys on her baby gym, the messaging system between her brain, eyes and arms will develop, allowing her to swipe at the dangling toys in one clean movement.

She will also start to judge distances as she swipes at the toys and misses, then gradually learns to do so with precision.

Introduces cause and effect

Your baby will start to realize that her movements can affect her world: for example, when she decides to swipe at a toy she can make it move, and perhaps cause it to make a noise. Likewise, if she tugs at the string of a helium balloon she will gradually realize that it is her movements making it move and that she is having an effect on the outside world.

15 Kick About

From about two months babies can kick very energetically as they begin to use their large muscles. It's beneficial for your baby to have some nappy-free time so that he's not restricted when he kicks; put his changing mat on the floor and an old clean towel underneath his bottom, just in case!

The bath is another great place for your baby to kick; lie him on his back in the water and carefully support his head. Put a reasonable amount of water in the bath – about 15 cm (6 in) – so there is enough for your baby to kick. You can encourage him to kick in the water by gently moving his legs – it may be useful to enlist another pair of hands to help with this.

What you need

Any of the following:
- Changing mat
- Clean nappy
- Bath
- Baby gym

NEW BABY

Your baby will enjoy the sensation of the water swishing against his legs and will probably start kicking on his own.

Your baby's legs will get stronger over the coming months and he will learn to kick with more precision; try putting his baby gym near his feet so he can get in some target practice. If you have a baby gym with added sound effects, your baby may find it easier to trigger the sounds with his feet than with his arms at first because his legs will be stronger (think of all the kicking practice he had in the womb).

You may also notice that, when your baby reaches about five months, he discovers his toes and starts to suck them. Give him plenty of time lying on a mat without his socks. You could also leave his socks off on the changing mat – an ideal toe-sucking opportunity.

Benefits

Preparation for first steps
Vigorous kicking aids the development of the gross motor skills and builds the large leg muscles that will eventually enable your baby to crawl and walk.

Relieves nappy rash
Any time spent without a nappy on is a big help if your baby suffers from nappy rash. As mentioned previously, five minutes will help and a couple of hours will make a dramatic difference.

Builds water confidence
Any bath-time games that your baby enjoys will teach him that water is fun and encourage a love of water in the future.

Teaches about cause and effect
Your baby will probably kick spontaneously in the bath and the harder he kicks, the more he will splash. When he realizes that it is his legs making the splashes, he will enjoy deliberately kicking as hard as he can as he learns that he not only has an impact on the world, but that it is fun, too.

This also applies when your baby kicks at his baby gym. As soon as he makes the connection between his kicking legs and the toys moving and perhaps making sounds, he will be encouraged to kick more. You may even notice him stopping and waiting, then starting to kick again as he experiments with cause and effect.

16 Nappy Fun

Many parents struggle to find time to play in the early months, but if you play a short game every time you change your baby's nappy, you'll soon clock up hours of playtime together. Pooey nappies do require some concentration, of course, but once she's clean and you're simply putting on a new nappy and getting her dressed again, it's easy enough to play.

Have fun blowing raspberries on her tummy – babies start to laugh from about three months, so she'll soon squeal with delight when you do

What you need

- Non-breakable mirror

this. You can also sing songs – make up a daft nappy song to sing each time you change your baby's nappy. She'll become familiar with it, especially if it includes simple actions. Perhaps you tickle her toes or blow on her nose. Blowing your baby's face is a fun thing to do during a nappy change, and it avoids touching her face and possibly spreading bacteria (*see right*).

Put a non-breakable mirror (plastic rather than glass) beside the changing mat so that your baby can have fun looking at her face. Mirrors reflect light, which even a new baby will enjoy.

Over the first few months you'll gradually get into a nappy-changing routine. If you stick to this every time, it will encourage cooperation once your baby is older, as small children find such routines very soothing.

Benefits

Encourages communication

Blowing raspberries, blowing gently in your baby's face and singing with your baby are all good ways to connect with her as you'll be making eye contact and watching closely for her reaction. Being sensitive to a child's response is fundamental to language development later on. Blowing has the added advantage of enhancing sensory development.

Builds neck muscles

If you put a mirror by the changing mat, your baby will turn her head to look at it, which will strengthen her neck muscles and improve head control.

Soothes

If nappy time becomes a fun routine that you share with your baby, she'll find it predictable and soothing. This will be particularly useful if she gets painful nappy rash, or when she gets a bit older and is more likely to become bored and object to lying still for her nappy change.

Reduces flattened head syndrome

If your baby tends to always sleep with her head on the same side, she may develop flattened head syndrome (*see page 17*). Putting a strategically placed mirror by the changing mat will encourage her to turn her head to the other side.

17 Shake that Rattle

From about three months your baby will have a little control over her arms, so try giving her a rattle to hold. She won't shake it at first but once she discovers that when she moves her arm the rattle makes a noise, she'll start to understand how it works and shake it more. A cloth rattle will be best because at this age your baby will be clumsy and may bash her head; plus, cloth rattles are lighter than plastic ones. Try to find a rattle that makes a sound at the slightest shake as this will be easiest for your baby to use.

What you need

- Soft fabric rattle

Coordination

As your baby practises shaking the rattle, her arm movements will become smoother and less jerky as the messaging system between her eyes, brain and arms becomes more efficient.

18 Tiger up a Tree

If you've been living with a colicky baby for the last few weeks, you may be desperate to quieten him when he's suffering from his colicky spasms (usually in the evenings). This activity may help. Hold him, tummy down, along your forearm with your hand under his chest, so that he resembles a tiger lying along the branch of a tree. You can use your other hand to rub his back and massage his tummy. Move him around the room for added excitement – the tree blows in the wind! This game seems to soothe most colicky babies to some extent.

What you need

- A forearm – the longer the better (a good one for dads)

What is colic?

Colic is a poorly understood condition that is defined by excessive and inconsolable crying in a baby that otherwise appears to be healthy and well fed. The crying usually lasts for more than three hours, beginning at about three weeks of age and easing by four to six months. Your baby will appear to be in pain and have a tight tummy.

Benefits

Relieves colic

Holding your baby in this way will soothe him because your arm is putting gentle pressure against his tummy. In addition, he will suddenly see the world from a new perspective and this can help distract him from his pain.

19 Face to Face

Your baby will love gazing at your face and, from about three months, she will start to enjoy playing with it. By this age she will be strong enough to hold her head up and look around the room when you carry her, and she will reach out and grab at her favourite toy – your face. Have fun together as she gets hold of your nose, mouth, tongue and ears (watch out for earrings; you may need to remove these, or at least avoid dangly ones for a few months). Your baby will be fascinated when you open and close your mouth, and put her hand on your lips as you hum so that she can feel

What you need

- Your face

Any of the following:

- Hat
- Unbreakable chunky necklace
- Old glasses

Benefits

Improves coordination

To tug at your ear or put her hand in your mouth, your baby needs to judge distance and coordinate her movement; then she needs the fine motor skills to grab her target.

Teaches the concept of 'other'

Newborn babies think they are part of their mother, gradually learning that they are a separate person. From four months your baby will learn that if she cries she gets your attention, rather than blindly crying for milk. This sense of self increases until, once she's a toddler, it becomes so strong that she insists on doing everything her own way. In the meantime, playing with your face will help your baby to learn where she ends and you begin. It's a great way to help her to develop her sense of independence and separateness.

Encourages social interaction

It's very important for your baby's social development that she interacts with her parents. She'll have a wonderful time playing with your face, and from around four months, when babies love smiling at those closest to them, will really respond to fun games like pulling your nose and ears. Faces are vital to good communication; your baby will be watching faces closely for the rest of her life, and early encouragement in this area will help her learn to read expressions accurately.

Promotes understanding of the world

Messing about with your face will teach your baby that mouths are wet, tongues stick out, hats and glasses come off and lips vibrate.

the vibrations. Also try blowing your cheeks out and teaching your baby to squash the air out with her fists to make a noise.

Try putting on a big sturdy necklace, a hat or old glasses and letting your baby grab at them (although, if you or anyone else close to your baby wears glasses you may want to avoid playing with glasses or she'll be forever pulling at the real thing).

20 First Conversations

From about three months, babies really begin to use their voice to make sounds other than crying, and by four months they often make sounds when you talk to them. Your baby may make simple sounds such as coo, goo, ka, da, ba, ma, na, and so on, and as he starts to enjoy his voice he will experiment with his vocal cords, making high- and low-

What you need
- A quiet place

pitched sounds – sometimes you'll hear strange squeals as your baby tries out a new noise.

Take a little time to sit and listen to your baby. You can do this whenever you are playing together, or even while you are giving him a bath or changing his nappy. You may have to wait a minute or two for him to find his voice but if you are patient he may eventually 'say' something. Repeat whatever sound he makes to encourage him to 'talk' more. You can also respond simply by looking him in the eye and nodding and smiling when he makes a sound. This shows that you are really listening – it's the beginning of a conversation. Try replying to your baby's chatter with something like, 'Ooh, is that right?' Chances are you'll find yourself speaking in a gentle, high-pitched voice when you talk to him – this is a natural response and has been shown to actually encourage babies to talk and learn language. Keep background noise to a minimum during this activity because babies aren't very good at separating one sound from another.

You can also sing songs with your baby; you may find that he joins in with his own sounds. Stop and listen to him and, when he's finished, praise him and repeat his sounds to encourage him to 'sing' more.

If your baby makes an extended 'aaaah' sound, put your hand over his open mouth and then lift it up and down to vary his sounds – he'll love this game once he gets the hang of it.

Benefits

Encourages your baby to use his voice

The more you respond positively to your baby's sounds, the more he will use his voice. This will give him lots of practice at using his vocal tract, which is controlled by eighty muscles – it takes a baby about a year to gain full control. By five months, babies have enough control to make sounds that actually resemble real language (although most babies don't say their first word until about one year).

Aids language development

Responding to your baby when he 'talks' is fundamental to his language development. By repeating sounds back to him and showing that you are listening to what he has to say, you will teach your baby the rudiments of conversation and show him that he can use his voice to communicate. This will have a positive impact on future language development and may encourage him to be an early talker.

21 Puppet Hands

At around four months your baby will discover her hands and start to play with them. She'll gaze at them, then be absolutely fascinated when they move. She'll touch her hands together and be amazed at the new sensation. You'll see her gradually gaining control over her hands as she learns to coordinate her movements.

To help your baby locate her hands more easily, you can make special gloves for her to wear. Cut the closed end off a pair of brightly coloured baby socks or scratch mittens, so that when you put them on her hands she can see her fingers. Then sew on bells securely around the wrist end – these will ring when your baby moves her hands and arms. Put just one glove on your baby to begin with. Her attention will naturally be drawn to the

What you need

- Brightly coloured baby socks or scratch mittens
- Bells
- Buttons
- Needle and thread
- Marker pen

Benefits

Improves hand–eye coordination
Your baby will want to watch the gloves or puppets moving on her hands, so she will learn to move her hands and head together, and this will help to develop her hand–eye coordination. When she wears the face puppets, she'll turn her hands to see the faces, which will further develop her coordination.

Promotes understanding of cause and effect
Your baby will soon learn that when she moves her hands the bells ring. She'll realize that she can control the sound and that by moving her hands she can make things happen – this is an important developmental step.

Provides entertainment
Babies are naturally entertained by their hands when they first discover them; it's as though they've been given brand-new toys to play with. But after a couple of weeks when the novelty wears off, putting on puppet socks gives their hands a new element of interest. You can pop these on at any time, and even keep a pair in the changing bag for when you're out and about. Your baby will be enthralled and have great fun playing with her hands all over again.

bright colours and the sound of the bells and she'll focus on this hand and move it more than her non-gloved hand. The following day you could put a glove on her other hand – you'll see her focus on this hand as she attempts to control and move it. Then put both the gloves on and watch her move her hands, waving them about separately and together, entwining and touching her fingers.

After a few weeks, when your baby has become familiar with her hands and the gloves, you could make mini puppets for her by sewing buttons securely onto a pair of baby socks or scratch mittens (without the toes or tops cut off) to make eyes and a nose, and using stitching or a marker pen for the mouth. A quicker option is to draw the complete face with a marker pen. When wearing the puppets, your baby will be fascinated by the face and will turn her hand to look at it and perhaps smile or babble to it.

22 Bouncing Baby

By around five months your baby may have enough head control for you to put him in a door bouncer, although some babies won't be ready for another month or so. A door bouncer is like a swing that is suspended from a doorway on elastic, and your baby is strapped into a harness low enough for his feet to touch the ground. The idea is that he can stand and, eventually, jump up and down. If your baby is particularly lively, he will soon learn to swing, turn around and even spin. Most babies love the excitement of standing upright and turning themselves around to look in every direction.

There is a knack to getting a baby into a bouncer so, to begin with, you may need someone to help; if it takes too long your baby will be put off before you even start. The first few times, put your baby in the harness for just five minutes, but, of course, take him out sooner if he becomes upset. Then, if he's happy, you can gradually build up to a maximum of twenty minutes. It may be tempting to leave him in his harness while you get on with your chores, but do ensure that you always stay in the same room so that

What you need

- Door bouncer

NEW BABY

you can keep an eye on him. If he starts to cry or seems unhappy in any way, take him out immediately because this probably means he's tired.

Once your baby is comfortable in his bouncer, you could give him a rattle to hold; he'll learn that by jumping up and down he can cause it to make a noise. You could also put a soft toy or a ball by his feet for him to kick.

Benefits

Strengthens neck and leg muscles

Being upright will mean your baby is using his neck muscles to support his head, so they will gradually become stronger. Because he is controlling his movement with his legs, he will also be working his leg muscles and building them up – great preparation for crawling and walking.

Encourages physical activity

If your baby is energetic, he will particularly enjoy being in a bouncer. At this age, babies aren't yet mobile, so there's not a great deal they can do to physically wear themselves out – apart from kick furiously when lying on their back or splash around in the bath or in a swimming pool (*see page 53*). You may find that your baby sleeps better than usual after a session in his bouncer because he has released all his pent-up energy. Once he's on the move, there will be no stopping him and he'll easily wear himself out.

Improves coordination and balance

As your baby is suspended he'll discover a sense of balance as he moves. This will develop as he learns how to jump and turn himself around, skills that will also improve his coordination. If you give him a ball to kick, he will practise controlling his feet.

Relieves reflux

Some babies are prone to reflux, with possetting being a main symptom. This tends to peak at about four months. Putting your baby in an upright position in his chair from time to time can be a very effective remedy for this.

23 Early Outings

In the first six months there's no need to go mad planning elaborate child-friendly outings for your baby because, at this age, any new environment will seem fascinating. If you did take your baby somewhere like the zoo, chances are she'd ignore the animals and become enthralled by something very mundane such as a trolley loaded up with brooms! It's far better to include her in lots of everyday trips out that she will find exciting because, for her, the world is still a very unfamiliar place. So, pack up her changing bag, ensure that she isn't tired and is well fed (or that you have bottles prepared or access to somewhere that is breast-feeding-friendly), then put her in the buggy and off you go.

If you take your baby to the supermarket when she's very little, she will probably fixate on the lights, then after a few months she'll start to enjoy the colours, the other shoppers and the checkout assistants. Public transport or a car journey will seem like a big adventure for your baby, who will be mesmerized by

What you need

- Changing bag
- Bottles of milk or a place to breastfeed

the moving scenery and the noise. If she's on a train or a bus, she'll be fascinated by the other passengers – and everyday things like escalators or automatic doors will seem like magic. She'll even enjoy clothes shopping, touching different fabrics and seeing herself in big mirrors. Whatever you decide to do, make sure you keep it fairly short so your baby doesn't become overwhelmed or bored.

One outing that *can* be centred around your baby in the early months is swimming, which you can do from as early as eight weeks. You could join a baby swim class, where she may even learn to swim under water for a few seconds. Or, simply have fun splashing about at your local pool.

Benefits

Improves understanding of the world

Much of what babies see in the early months is new and, although they can't speak, you will notice that your baby seems particularly fascinated and alert if she goes somewhere new. She's taking everything in and learning about how the world works, and exploring her environment with her eyes will enhance her cognitive development (thinking skills). Seeing new things and new people is very stimulating and you'll probably find that your baby becomes more tired than usual.

Promotes socializing

All kinds of people will coo at your baby in the early months and make a fuss of her. She's too young to be stranger-phobic, which doesn't develop before eight months, so she'll delight in grinning away at everyone she sees.

Encourages listening

Your baby will notice all kinds of sounds: the hiss of a coffee machine in a café; the beeping of traffic lights; the slam of a car door. Hearing a variety of different noises will enhance your baby's auditory processing skills as her brain gradually works out where these sounds are coming from, whether they are soft, loud, high or low, what they mean and how she should react.

Builds water confidence

Just splashing about will teach your baby to love water, but if she also learns to hold her breath and swim under water, this could save her life if she were ever to fall into water – it would buy her a few vital seconds.

24 Music Time

What you need

- A radio or music player

Countless studies have shown that babies can benefit from hearing classical music. Tune into a classical music station on the radio, or dig out your own selection, then make a point of listening together. You could also pick your baby up and dance; he will love it if you hold him while waltzing around the room. If you play a musical instrument, you could practise near your baby and see what he makes of it.

Keep music sessions with your baby short and focused. It's best not to have background music on too often, especially if you're talking to your baby. Babies struggle to screen out background noise and, if there's always a radio or television on, it could interfere with language development.

Safety first

Babies' ears are sensitive to loud noise; always ensure that the volume is never so high that you have to raise your voice to speak.

Although it used to be thought that exposure to classical music could boost a baby's IQ, experts no longer believe this to be the case. However, there is little doubt that music has a profound effect on a baby's development, particularly classical music because its complex structure appears to stimulate the brain and affect the way neurological pathways are laid down. Now research suggests that other music can affect babies too. In a study published in the journal *Proceedings of the National Academy of Sciences*, five-month-old babies were found to move rhythmically when they heard music, and it was the beat rather than the melody that stimulated this response. The study showed that the more rhythmically the babies were able to move, the more they smiled. So if classical music isn't your thing, don't worry. Switch on your favourite tunes and have fun dancing with your baby, or let him lie on his play mat and kick his legs and wave his arms to the beat. Help him to move in time to the music and he'll start to feel the rhythm and really enjoy it.

Benefits

Has a calming effect

Classical music can calm babies because it stimulates the brain's alpha waves, which have a soothing effect. One study published in the journal *Pediatrics* showed that pre-term babies who listened to Mozart felt calmer and so expended less energy, which increased their growth. Some experts in previous studies have speculated that the beat of Mozart's music can be compared to a mother's heartbeat, which is why babies find it so calming. Other studies have found that if babies listen to music with a slow beat, it can actually decrease their heart rate and slow their breathing, helping them to relax.

Helps develop language

Listening to classical music can help your baby to develop his auditory memory and improve his ability to decode the sounds that he hears. He'll need these same skills as he learns to listen to and understand language.

Uplifts your baby's mood

A joyful piece of classical music will cause the body to produce endorphins, feel-good chemicals that are released in the brain. These will not only boost your baby's mood, but will also help him to relax. Plus, it will have the same effects on you, helping you to feel more relaxed and happy, which is great for both you and your baby.

25 Baby Blast-off

From about four months it will no longer be necessary to carefully support your baby's head when you hold him, or handle him like a breakable antique. In fact you can be quite boisterous with him and introduce a bit of rough and tumble – this is where dad really comes into his own.

By now, babies are able to lift their head and shoulders when they are lying on their tummy, and by the time they get to five months they have the strength to lift their head when they are lying on their back. This increased neck control means that you can bounce your baby on your knee, whizz him up high and even do a 'baby blast-off', launching him into the air and perching him on a high shelf or on top of the fridge – holding him safely throughout, of course. Then you can sing 'Humpty Dumpty sat

What you need

- High surface
- Double bed or duvet

on a wall, Humpty Dumpty had a great fall ...' and zoom him downwards as you pretend he's falling.

Another fun game is to lie on your back with your knees bent and together, making a platform with your shins on which to lie your baby on his tummy and facing you. Hold his arms to keep him stable, then gently raise your feet towards the ceiling so that your baby's head tips towards you. As you both become used to the movement, you can move your legs faster and further – your baby will love tipping backwards and forwards.

Roly-poly is also fun to play at this age. Simply lie your baby on a double bed, or on a duvet on the floor, and roll him across it one way, then back the other way.

Watch your baby's mood

Not all babies like rough-and-tumble games, and some babies have days when they love such games and other days when they don't want to play. Be guided by your baby and don't force him to play if he seems upset.

Benefits

Aids social development

Dads tend to play with their babies differently to moms: dads are more likely to whizz their babies in the air and engage in rough-and-tumble activities, whereas moms tend to play in a gentler and quieter way. Babies notice the difference in how mom and dad interact with them from an early age and this teaches them that men and women are different.

Boosts interaction and bonding

Physical play is fun for both you and your baby and will deepen your bond with your child.

Helps muscle development

Your baby will need good neck control as he is whizzed and bounced about, and this will help to strengthen his neck muscles.

Aids development of the vestibular system

This is the part of the brain that controls balance and, once it has developed, we can jump up and down knowing that it is us that are moving and not our surroundings. Babies love to be swung around and rocked, and some experts think this is nature's way of helping the vestibular system to develop.

Part Two

Older Baby
Six to Twelve Months

It's amazing how much babies change during their first six months. Already your tiny newborn has turned into a big, bouncing baby who can giggle and wriggle with gusto. He's going to continue to change at an incredible rate, so you'll need to keep pace when it comes to playing to ensure that you match his developmental needs.

Now your baby is six months old he can chuckle and grab toys, has good control of his head and neck and is very inquisitive. Soon he'll be sitting up and, before you know it, he'll be on the move. It's going to be an exciting time and there are plenty of ways to have fun with your baby at this age. As you'll be weaning your baby around now, we've explained how mealtimes can be turned into fun activities. And by about eleven months your little one will start to show that he has a sense of humour. You'll soon find out that sharing a joke with your baby can be the most wonderfully bonding experience, and we'll show you how.

On the move

Once your baby discovers mobility, he'll start to move around a little by rolling over and will eventually start to crawl. We've included plenty of activities to encourage him to practise, and also to build up strength in preparation for being on the move. Do note that some babies never crawl but, instead, get about by bottom shuffling, which is perfectly normal. If this sounds like your baby, you can still play the crawling games with him but he will simply bottom shuffle instead.

If your baby is particularly advanced, he may stand before he is one and perhaps even walk. If this is the case, you may want to look at the next section for some play ideas for babies who are cruising (walking around with support).

More playtime

The next six months is a really fun time to play with your baby and you'll see him take some huge developmental leaps as he prepares to walk and talk. He'll be less sleepy than he used to be and will be more willing to play – play will become an increasingly important part of his life. He'll also be able to play for longer and you can expect him to be content with focusing on one activity for up to about fifteen minutes before wanting to move on to something else.

Go with the flow

You are bound to find that on some days your baby is delighted to join in with singing sessions or be pushed on the swings in the park, but on other days he'll be fretful and not very interested in playing. It is normal at this age for your baby to have days when he doesn't want to play, and the most likely reason is because he is teething or coming down with a cold. When you are having a non-play day, just go with it and cuddle your baby as much as is practical. You can also look through our suggestions and pick out the quieter, gentler activities such as reading stories together or looking at family photos.

Another new stage that will occur in the coming six months is that your baby will start to have an opinion of his own and will make it very clear if he doesn't like something. Be sensitive to what your baby wants and if you discover that he likes some of our suggested activities more than others, it's fine for him to play these over and over again. If he's happy, he will be benefitting far more than if he's being cajoled into doing something simply because you think it is 'good for him'.

There are countless ways to have fun with your baby during this phase, and each of our activities is not only designed to be entertaining for both you and your child, but will help him to progress through his milestones too.

26 Peekaboo!

In its simplest form, catch your baby's eye, cup your hands over your face, and then open them suddenly saying 'peekaboo!' or 'boo!'. Once your child reaches about ten months, she will be old enough to hide behind her hands and say 'peekaboo' back to you. Or you could put a cloth or towel over her head then take it off and say 'boo'. Alternating who says 'boo' will give her an early lesson in taking turns.

What you need

- An expressive face
- Something to hide behind, for example your hands, a door, a cushion or a piece of clothing.

Benefits

Teaches object permanence

If you play peekaboo with your baby, once she is eight months or older she will anticipate you saying 'boo' or 'peekaboo', and she will giggle as she waits for you to appear from behind your hands or the door. Younger than this and you will find that she has no expectation because she hasn't yet developed object permanence so thinks that if she can't see something or someone it simply doesn't exist.

Relieves separation anxiety

Peekaboo can help to teach babies that their mother can disappear then reappear again. Separation anxiety peaks from eight months to three years, which makes children very clingy – perhaps crying if mom leaves the room. Because peekaboo makes a game out of mom disappearing, it can help babies learn to cope with their separation anxiety. Before babies are able to understand object permanence they won't cry if mom goes away – out of sight out of mind.

Helps baby cope with fear

This is where dad comes into his own. If you make peekaboo a bit scary – roaring when you appear instead of a mild 'boo' – your child will jump. Then as she becomes used to the game she will squeal excitedly when dad appears, knowing that even though she feels a little afraid she is also safe and loved.

Teaches ordering and sequencing

Your baby will soon learn the order of peekaboo. Mom hides, she waits, then mom reappears. This teaches your baby about sequences and ordering as she learns the pattern of events.

Why children cling

It's normal for children to be clingy and stranger-phobic between the ages of eight months and three years. It shows that they have a close loving relationship with mom, so don't worry if you can't walk across the room without your child hanging onto your legs for security. Paediatricians worry slightly if children of stranger-phobic age show no concerns with strangers and are happy to come up and be friendly. This can indicate that their relationship with mom isn't close.

27 Enjoy a Song

Babies love to sing. Your baby will enjoy listening to you sing and also joining in with simple songs by making noises. You may already know some nursery rhymes, in which case start to sing them with your baby, if you haven't done so already. But if you can't quite remember the words you sang as a child, or need a few ideas, you can buy or borrow nursery-rhyme books or CDs, search for songs on the internet or join a baby-and-toddler group that focuses on singing nursery rhymes, where you can learn new songs with your baby – not to mention some great actions!

Sit your baby on your knee and bounce him up and down as you sing; by six months he'll have the strength to hold his head up quite easily. By about seven months he will

What you need

- Book of nursery rhymes
- Nursery-rhyme CD
- Scarf or tea towel
- Cuddly toy animals

be able to sit on the floor while you sing. You can also sit on the floor facing each other, then hold your baby's hands – try 'rowing a boat' together. From around nine months, babies are old enough to start following simple actions such as clapping, waving, nodding their heads or flapping their arms like wings. You'll have to be patient; expect it to take a little while for your baby to learn such actions. The best way to teach him is little and often.

Using props during your singing sessions can be great fun. If you're singing about a bear, try to find a teddy bear to hold while you sing. Or play tug-of-war with a tea towel; your baby can sit on the floor and pull, and you can make up a pirate song about pulling ropes and heaving up the anchor and so on. Making up songs can be great fun; it really doesn't matter if they're not very good as only your baby will hear, and he will think your songs are wonderful! Try inventing songs for nappy changing, going in the buggy, bath time and any other everyday activity. Just try to remember the songs from day to day so that they become familiar to your baby.

Benefits

Boosts language and memory

Babies are able to memorize songs long before they can remember spoken language. This is because it's actually easier for them to recognize a melody than a series of words. A word like 'sleep', for example, is a single syllable but it has four sounds within it – 's', 'l', 'ee' and 'p'. This is much more complicated than a single note of music, so learning a melody actually helps babies to learn the words of a song. You may find that, in time, your child can sing a phrase of a song long before he is able to put more than two words of speech together.

In addition, doing actions and using props enhances the memory and will help your child to remember the words more easily.

Improves balance and muscle strength

Sitting on the floor and clapping his hands will encourage your baby to use his abdominal muscles for balance rather than his arms. The song 'Row, row, row the boat' is good for balance and will help him to use his core muscles. Playing tug-of-war when he's sitting will also improve his balance as well as boosting upper-body strength, which he will need when pulling himself up to standing.

28 Roly-poly

Your baby may have rolled from her tummy to her back as early as four months and will probably roll from her back to her front at around six months. Being able to roll both ways means that your baby can potentially do roly-polies across the floor, which gives her great mobility, especially once she learns to steer.

You can encourage rolling by waving a toy to the side that she normally leans towards. If she reaches far enough to try to get it, she may roll over. If she has mastered front-to-back rolling, start when she is on her front as she will find this way easiest. You can also use this trick to encourage her to roll in her non-favourite direction. Once she gets the hang of this game, put your baby on her back and wave the toy to encourage her to roll onto her front.

What you need

- A soft surface
- A few toys

It's also fun to roll with your baby. You'll soon discover that it's far more comfortable to roll on carpet and grass than on a hard floor – do bear this in mind when you are encouraging your baby to roll. She may also like to practise rolling in her cot which, again, is soft but also has some grip, like carpet, which makes learning to roll easier.

Once your baby is able to roll both ways and is mobile, you can have fun putting objects just out of her reach and encouraging her to roll over. Do stop this game if she becomes frustrated – simply pass her the toy as she won't gain anything from being forced to try to reach it. If you try again in a week or so, you may well see a big improvement in her rolling skills – babies develop quickly at this age.

Safety first

Once your baby becomes mobile, you will need to be even more vigilant about safety. Ensure that there's no possibility of her rolling down the stairs, or even down one step. Don't leave small objects lying around, such as coins or pen lids, that she may put in her mouth. Also, secure any wobbly furniture that she may roll into, and put away anything potentially dangerous such as plastic bags, bits of string or vases that may topple onto her if she rolls into them. Always over-estimate how far your baby can roll – lots of parents are very surprised at how quickly babies learn this skill. And, it goes without saying, never leave your baby on a changing table or bed as she's bound to fall off now that she can roll.

Benefits

Teaches about weight transfer
Rolling teaches babies to transfer their weight from side to side, a skill that is essential for crawling.

Provides entertainment
Your baby will get a big thrill from rolling. The sensation of moving her entire body by herself will be very exciting and she'll suddenly see the world from a different perspective.

Helps build muscle strength
Rolling uses the abdominal muscles, particularly when your baby rolls from her back to her front. Building these muscles will make sitting and crawling easier. Rolling also builds neck and arm muscles which will help with crawling.

29 Book Worm

Six months of age (or thereabouts) is a lovely time to start reading with your baby, if you haven't done so already. We mentioned sharing textured books with your baby during his first six months (*see activity 11, Touchy Feely*). Now, between about six and eight months, he will be ready to start looking at and enjoying some non-touch board books. These are sturdy enough for him to grab and chew without being destroyed.

Choose picture books with one-word labels, or very simple stories with short sentences. Also choose books with large, clear pictures because at this age a baby's eyesight isn't developed enough to appreciate small details and pale colours.

Start by looking at the pictures together; your baby may find the story difficult to understand if you simply read the text and will lose interest. Go at your baby's pace, so if he wants to linger

What you need

- Simple stories and picture books

on one particular picture then let him. Some days he may become fascinated with turning the pages back and forth and not really want to dwell on any of the pictures, and that's fine too. He may want to keep looking at the same book again and again – this may be boring for you but your baby will be finding the familiarity very comforting, so bear with him if you can.

Your aim at this stage should be to teach your child to love books. Don't make it too educational; there's plenty of time for learning and he'll learn much faster in the future if he feels happy and comfortable around books. Don't even think about letter recognition or learning to read, and resist the temptation to try to explain anything too complicated for the time being – keep things light and fun. Having lots of books in your home will help, especially if your child sees you reading them. Let him 'play' with the book on your bedside table and, if you're flicking through a cookery book, show him the pictures. Your baby is still too young to point out and label pictures in books, so don't ask 'Where's the cat?' because at this age you will be wasting your time. Keep things fun and simple, and spend just a few minutes at a time looking at books together.

Benefits

Boosts language development
Babies learn the meaning of lots of words long before they are able to speak, so as you chatter away about pictures in your baby's books, it will help improve his vocabulary.

Teaches about two dimensional and three dimensional
At first your baby may see an object – an apple, perhaps – on a page, then when you turn the page he will turn it back and try to find the item he's just seen. Understanding that pictures are two dimensional and that you can't actually hold them is a big developmental leap. Be patient when your baby insists on turning the pages back and forth over and over again.

Demonstrates how books work
As your baby becomes familiar with books he'll start to understand that you hold them upright and turn the pages from right to left (but read the pages from left to right) and that stories have a beginning and an end. He'll also learn that the cover tells you what the book is about. This is such obvious stuff for adults but, to a baby who is unfamiliar with books, it's an important part of his learning.

30 Food Play

From around six months your baby will start to try solid food and will be experiencing all kinds of new flavours and textures. It's normal for babies to want to experiment with their food, squeezing, smearing and eventually throwing it (expect the latter from about eleven months). Playing with food is good for development and meals should be a game. Your baby will be driven by curiosity about textures as well as tastes, so let her squelch and squeeze her food in her hands.

You can give your baby a spoon at any age, although she won't make much progress with using it until at least nine months and then you will have to load her spoon for her and help guide it into her mouth. In the meantime you can give your baby lots of interesting finger foods to play with: for example, pasta shapes, noodles, slices of hard-boiled egg, broccoli. She'll have a wonderful time touching, gumming and perhaps even eating them. Give her a selection of food on a plate, or her highchair tray, and let the fun begin. Try to resist the temptation to wipe up the mess, including your baby's face, until the end of the meal – she'll see clean-up attempts as an irritating interruption to her play.

From about nine months your baby will develop the pincer grip, so she'll be able to pick up tiny objects between her thumb and forefinger. This means you can give her things like peas and halves of blueberry to try to feed to herself.

Many parents find the early months of weaning quite stressful because there is a lot of mess and waste.

Benefits

Reduces the risk of food anxiety

Lots of food hang-ups in children occur because parents try to control mealtimes too much, perhaps trying to make their little one eat more or minimize the mess. Babies soon try to resist this control, which can result in mealtime battles and refusal to eat very much. Allowing your baby to play with food forces you to be more relaxed and this has an extremely positive effect on your baby's attitude to food.

She'll be happy and calm at mealtimes and will be far more likely to grow up with a healthy relationship with food.

Improves dexterity

Once your baby has developed the pincer grip, practising this skill will greatly develop her dexterity. It's much safer to practise with little bits of food than other small objects that your baby could potentially choke on.

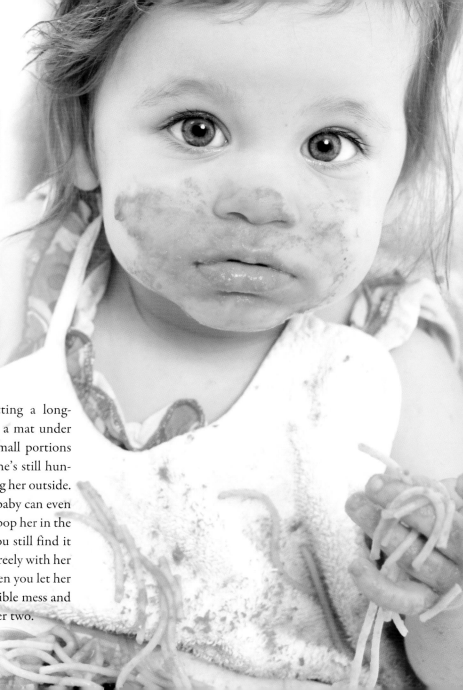

What you need

- A variety of finger foods
- A coverall bib

Safety first

Children under five shouldn't be given nuts as they present a choking hazard. Foods such as grapes and cherries should be cut in half (and any stones removed) as they could block the wind pipe.

To minimize the stress, try putting a long-sleeved coverall bib on your baby, a mat under the highchair and only give her small portions (you can always give her more if she's still hungry). If it's warm enough, try feeding her outside. For her final meal of the day your baby can even eat in just her nappy, then you can pop her in the bath soon after she's finished. If you still find it very difficult to let your baby play freely with her food, try having one meal a day when you let her play with her food and make a terrible mess and take a bit more control for the other two.

31 Toys with Buttons

From around six months, as your baby's vision improves, he'll be able to enjoy more complex toys such as those with buttons to press, handles to wind and dials to turn, and from around eight months he will enjoy making things happen. Initially you will have to help your baby play with such toys; then, as he gets the idea, he will love making the toy 'do' something. There are lots of these toys available – a Jack-in-the-box is the classic – or you could make one yourself. See opposite for how to make a Jack-in-the-box: the teddy pops up when you push the pencil, then disappears again when you pull it. Your baby will be fascinated to see how it works – take the time to explain the mechanism to him.

What you need

Any of the following:

- Baby-friendly toys with buttons to press and handles to wind
- Jack-in-the-box
- Small bucket
- String
- Small soft toy such as a teddy
- Sharp pencil
- Paper cup
- Tiny teddy or finger puppet
- Sticky tape

Another game that uses a pulling mechanism is teddy in a bucket – again, you can make this yourself. Tie some string to the handle of a toy bucket, then put the string over the top of a door and let the bucket dangle down the other side. When you pull the string, the bucket goes up. Encourage your baby to put a small soft toy into the bucket, then wave goodbye as you pull the string and the toy goes up in the bucket. As you lower the bucket again your baby can wave hello. Show him how it works and let him help you to pull and release the string. Even if your baby is too young to understand exactly how it works, he'll get the general idea.

Safety first

Never leave your baby alone with string.

To make your own Jack-in-the-box

Using a sharp pencil, make a hole in the bottom of a large paper cup (a cardboard cup from a coffee shop is ideal). Push the pencil through the cup, then securely attach a small soft toy, such as a teddy or finger puppet, with sticky tape – this will cover the sharp end of the pencil.

Benefits

Improves manual dexterity
Pushing buttons, pulling string and winding handles all require fine motor skills. Your baby will have fun perfecting these tiny movements if he's playing with fun toys.

Teaches about anticipation
A classic Jack-in-the-box is still probably the best toy for this because your baby won't be sure exactly when Jack will pop up. He'll know that by winding the handle the box plays a tune and that Jack will definitely pop up at some stage but, because he doesn't know exactly when, it will make the waiting very exciting.

Demonstrates cause and effect
With time, your baby will have control over these toys and will love being in charge of what happens. For example, he'll learn that if he presses a particular button an elephant pops up. With the homemade toys, he'll be able to see exactly how they work and eventually understand what causes the puppet to pop out of the cup and what makes the bucket go up and down.

32 Peekaboo Puppets

Your baby will be mesmerized and probably very excited if a favourite puppet or toy happens to appear over the side of her cot – or from behind a chair – and starts talking to her. Put a blanket or sheet over one end of the cot so that she can't see you if you crouch down. You could also crouch behind a sofa or a chair with a blanket or sheet over the back. Then, using either a glove puppet or a cuddly toy, make the character appear over the side of the cot and say 'hello' to your baby in a squeaky voice. She may crawl towards it and perhaps even pull herself up to standing to try to grab the puppet. If the character has a toy to give your baby, this will certainly encourage her to try to make her way across the cot. The puppet

What you need

- Two glove puppets or cuddly toys
- Small toy
- Blanket or sheet

could say, 'I've got a lovely little car, brrm brrm. Do you want to have a turn?'

Try showing your baby two puppets at once and making them talk to each other, perhaps even acting out a familiar scenario: 'I've shut my finger in the door, boo hoo.' 'Oh dear, kiss it better.'

Another fun game is 'boo'. Make the puppet disappear behind the blanket, then reappear and say 'boo'. Your baby will delight in this now that she is old enough to appreciate peekaboo games.

Eventually you can show your baby that it's you holding the puppet. She won't mind or be disappointed and will be just as enchanted by the puppet show next time it comes to town.

Benefits

Boosts concentration

Your baby will watch and listen as the puppets perform and, as she becomes involved in what they have to say, she will focus and concentrate. This will also improve her listening skills, although she will find it more difficult to understand the puppets than real people because babies rely on lip-reading in the early stages of language development.

Aids understanding of the world

Your baby will think the puppet is alive when it first appears but, when she sees you, she'll begin to understand how puppets work.

Helps develop conversation skills

Watching two puppets talk to each other will help your baby to understand how a conversation works, with people taking turns to talk. She will also become familiar with the rhythm of conversation and the length of the pauses in between speech. As your child gets older, she may even learn to use the puppet to talk about any traumatic issues: puppets are often used in play therapy to help children deal with difficult emotions and events.

Provides entertainment

Puppets are fun for babies to watch, and your baby will be fascinated and probably amused by this game, especially if the characters do something funny like sneeze and fall over (highly entertaining for most babies).

33 Roll the Ball

Babies love playing with balls, and from about six months they are capable of grabbing moving objects because they have the skills to work out how quickly and in what direction the object is moving. So, during tummy time, if you roll a ball to your baby he will be able to swipe at it with his arm. Use a light-weight, soft ball because your baby is bound to miss from time to time and the ball will bash into him. For variation, you could screw up some news-paper into balls and roll those towards your baby to swipe at or grab. You can also roll up a large piece of tinfoil – your baby will love the shininess. Do make sure it is too big for him to put in his mouth.

What you need

Any of the following:

- Soft beach ball
- Newspaper
- Tinfoil
- Toys with wheels

Once your baby is able to sit up without support (usually from around seven or eight months), he'll be able to play this game sitting up. From this position he is more likely to be able to roll the ball back to you. He will use a kind of patting action on the ball, and the direction it rolls in is down to chance rather than skill. Do give your baby lots of encouragement if he has a try, and show him how to pat the ball to you. If you continue playing these kinds of games with your baby once he is crawling, he'll have lots of fun trying to reach the ball.

You could also use toys on wheels to play this game; gently direct one towards your baby. Start with fairly large toys as these will be easier to push. He won't be able to push them back to you at first, but may have fun trying.

Benefits

Improves hand–eye coordination
From six months your baby's movements will become smoother so, rather than reaching for things jerkily, he will swipe smoothly as he reaches for a ball. Swiping at a moving ball will need quite refined hand–eye coordination skills because he will have to judge where the ball will be in a few seconds. He will learn to anticipate movement – both the direction and the speed at which an object is travelling. Toys with wheels will also help your baby develop this skill.

Teaches about anticipation
As your baby learns about movement he'll be able to calculate exactly when the ball will reach him. He'll get excited when he knows that you are about to roll the ball to him and he learns to anticipate that this is about to happen.

Improves balance
When your baby is sitting, he will turn from the waist to reach the ball and this will help develop his balancing skills. Also, if he takes his hands off the floor to grab at the ball, this will demonstrate even better balance because he won't be propping himself up with his hands. Being able to sit without having his hands on the floor is an important milestone for your baby as it will enable him to sit up and play with toys.

Encourages crawling
Playing with a ball encourages mobility as your baby will want to crawl towards the ball.

34 Brush-a-bye Baby

Take a soft brush, then gently brush your baby's arms and legs using a long sweeping action from her fingers to the tops of her arms and back again, then from her toes to the tops of her legs and back again. You can also brush her back. Brush therapists use a soft scrubbing brush – the type surgeons use to clean their hands – but a soft paintbrush or baby hairbrush is fine if you can't get hold of one.

Don't brush the tummy, chest or face because babies can sometimes find this unsettling. The pressure you use shouldn't be tickly, but neither should it be at all rough – aim for somewhere in between.

Brushing is a known therapeutic technique used on children to help with all kinds of problems, including attention deficit disorder, autism, learning difficulties and tactile defensiveness – which means a child finds it upsetting to be touched.

What you need

- Baby hairbrush
- Soft paintbrush

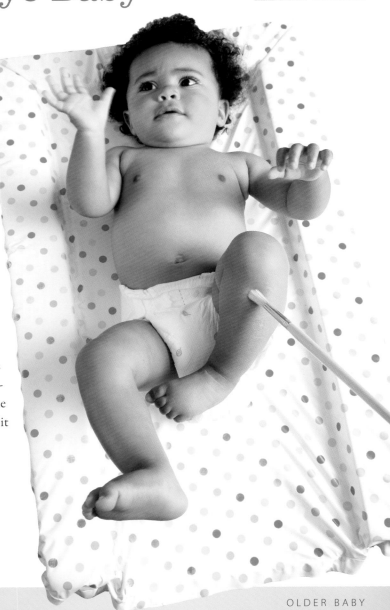

OLDER BABY

The theory behind why brush therapy works is all to do with a baby's primitive reflexes, such as the grasp-and stepping reflexes. If everything goes to plan, these reflexes should gradually disappear in the early months and years, to be replaced by controlled voluntary movements. However, sometimes these early survival reflexes are retained, which interferes with the development of controlled movement and can result in learning difficulties. Brushing is thought to help redress this balance because it stimulates specific nerve endings, which kick-starts the developmental process. It also activates outdated reflexes in order to shut them down.

If you suspect a problem such as any of those mentioned above, please seek professional help; we don't suggest you use this brushing game for therapeutic purposes. However, we do encourage you to brush your baby from time to time, simply because, like massage, it's a pleasant sensation and will stimulate your baby's sense of touch.

You can brush your baby at any time, but following a bath or nappy change are good times to try, when your baby isn't wearing too many clothes. Just a few minutes of brushing is sufficient– your baby will soon let you know if she's had enough, perhaps by fussing or turning her head away from you. Some babies won't like brushing and that's fine. There's no need to worry at this early stage that your baby is tactile defensive.

Benefits

Increases self-awareness
Brushing will help your baby to become more aware of the space that her body occupies as she focuses on each of her limbs while it is being brushed.

Improves coordination and movement
Brushing encourages the central nervous system to use information from the peripheral nervous system more effectively. This improves the way the brain and body work together as the brain learns to organize sensory information, helping your baby to become more coordinated and better at moving.

Encourages relaxation
Just as a massage helps babies to relax, brushing will have a calming effect as it's a very pleasurable experience. It should be very soothing for your baby, while at the same time possibly enhancing development.

35 Out and About

From six months your baby will be old enough to appreciate the unfamiliar, so when you go somewhere that he hasn't been before he'll find it very exciting. A trip on a bus or a train to somewhere quite mundane like the shops will seem like a stimulating day out for your baby. He will also enjoy accompanying you to the dentist or optician. If you can leave him in his buggy where he can see you, he'll probably be sufficiently entertained by what is going on not to want to get out. Some babies will be less content and won't be so easy to take around with you as you go about your day, but a little bag of toys or a few rice cakes (or other age-

What you need

- Well-stocked changing bag
- Spare clothes
- Bottle of milk and a snack
- Little bag of toys

OLDER BABY

appropriate snacks that you know your baby will cope with easily) will certainly help if your baby becomes restless.

Take the time to explain to your baby what is going on. He'll not only find this reassuring as a dentist peers into your mouth or the lights dim and an optician examines your eyes, but he'll also understand a little of what is happening and will be interested.

If your baby is already crawling and active, let him have a good crawl before you set off on a trip so that he's more likely to be happy to stay in his buggy. It's also worth timing such a trip carefully; by six months many babies are settled in a daytime napping routine so you could try to plan your outing not to clash with his sleep times.

As well as accompanying you on everyday excursions, you could also arrange some baby-centred outings. In Part One (activity 23, Early Outings) we mentioned swimming, which is an excellent thing to do with your baby if you haven't done so already. From about eight months you could also visit soft-play centres which often have areas designated for the under twos. By now your baby may also be able to appreciate places such as aquariums, farms and zoos; if there's a petting area you could even encourage him to touch the animals or give them some food. Of course, this will be easier once he is able to stand and walk, but still possible if he's in his buggy sitting up.

Safety first

Always wash both your baby's hands and your hands after touching farm animals.

Benefits

Promotes fun

When your baby is old enough to enjoy trips out, he'll have a lot of fun and so will you. Doing things that are unfamiliar will encourage his sense of adventure and hopefully boost his confidence.

Develops language

If you chatter to your baby about what's going on, it will help his language development and boost his understanding. You may be more likely to chat to him when you're out and about than at home when you may be trying to get things done.

Boosts understanding of the world

Although babies under one year don't say more than a word or two, they still understand a lot of what is happening and will absorb lots of information about what they see.

36 Mommy's Helper

From around seven months your baby will be old enough to enjoy 'helping' you. She'll observe you closely and want to join in with all kinds of things, so start taking the time to lift her out of her buggy to post letters and ring doorbells. At home your baby can switch lights on; she'll switch them on and off repeatedly, which doesn't really matter – she'll only do this under supervision as she won't be able to reach the switch by herself.

Benefits

Boosts understanding of the world
Your baby will learn what doorbells and light switches are for and also come to understand more about cause and effect.

Aids language development
If you're taking the time to involve your baby in simple tasks, you'll no doubt be talking to her about what she is doing, and this will help develop her understanding and vocabulary even before she starts talking.

Safety first
Check that your baby's fingers are dry before you let her touch a light switch.

What you need
- A few minutes when carrying out simple tasks

37 Go for a Swing

From around eight months most babies can sit unsupported and will enjoy going on a baby swing at the park (the ones with bars around the seat to stop them falling out). You'll find that, if your baby loves being rocked and bounced up and down in your arms, she will love the swings.

Sit your baby in the swing and show her how to hold the supporting bars with her hands. Gently push her from the front so that she can see you. Say 'weee' as she moves, or 'hello' as she swings towards you and 'bye bye' as she swings away from you (it's best not to wave at her or she may copy and wave back, and so let go of the swing).

What you need

- A local play area

Benefits

Improves balance

Repetitive movement is thought to stimulate the vestibular system – the part of the brain that senses balance and movement. A better sense of balance will help with crawling and walking.

38 Crawling Olympics

Even before your baby is crawling you can encourage him to get into the crawling position by putting a pillow under his tummy when he's lying down and placing his hands and knees on the floor. Once he is crawling by himself, make things fun by creating a crawling obstacle course. You can arrange piles of pillows for him to climb over, add sofa cushions to make an even bigger heap and cover this with a duvet – he may crawl around it or over it. Perhaps put a toy at the top for him to climb up and retrieve. Do check that your cushion monument is stable and won't collapse. Try putting a toy

What you need

Any of the following:

- Pillows
- Sofa cushions
- Duvets
- Cardboard boxes
- Small toys
- Plastic colander

on the other side of the 'mountain', then see if your baby climbs over to get it, or realizes that he can get the toy more easily simply by crawling around the pile of cushions.

You could also make a tunnel out of cardboard boxes opened up at each end, or leave one end sealed and see if your baby will crawl into the 'cave'.

Spend some time crawling with your baby; you'll be surprised at how tiring this is, but it will really encourage him to have fun and he'll love the fact that you're joining in. If you crawl up and down the room as fast as you can, he'll soon be racing along with you. Sharing silly time together is good for bonding – the sillier the better – so put a plastic colander on your head while you crawl, then let your baby have a turn.

It's also fun to let your baby crawl over you; pretend to be asleep, then wake up and growl when he's climbed onto you and lift him up onto your bent knees. This is a good game for dad, who may have some ideas of his own to add to those given here.

Benefits

Tires baby out
Enjoying lots of physical activity will help to increase your baby's appetite, which is helpful during the weaning months, and will also boost his fitness and wear him out so that, hopefully, he will sleep well both at night and at nap time.

Improves fitness
Before babies crawl they aren't particularly mobile, so encouraging your baby to crawl early is a good opportunity for some physical exertion, which will help boost his fitness. It will also help to strengthen his arms, legs, back and tummy in preparation for standing and walking.

Improves balance
To keep the colander on his head, your baby will need to balance it and this will require good neck control. He will also learn how to control his speed so the colander doesn't fall off.

Teaches how to cope with failure
When the colander does fall off, you can laugh, to show that it's all right when things go wrong. Make a point of letting the colander fall off your head too and laughing about it together.

39 Making Music

We talked about playing music and singing to your baby in activities 24 (Music Time) and 27 (Enjoy a Song) and now it's time for your baby to start making her own music. From around eight months, babies start to bang surfaces using their hands, and your little one may sometimes bang her highchair tray. Encourage your baby to do this; perhaps sing to her rhythm or bang a work surface and play along with her. You could even put on some music for your baby to accompany her rhythmic banging.

Encourage her to play music in other ways: give her a cardboard box to

What you need

Any of the following:

- Cardboard box
- Toy drum
- Rings with bells
- Clear water bottle
- Dried lentils
- Rice
- Wooden spoon
- Saucepans

bang with her hands, or a toy drum (bear in mind that this will be a little noisier!); you can buy rings with bells attached, which make a lot of noise but don't require too much strength to shake; or you could fill an empty plastic bottle with rice or dried lentils for your baby to shake – use a small bottle and don't overfill or it will be too heavy for your baby to lift.

As your baby becomes more dexterous you could give her a wooden spoon to use as a makeshift drumstick and show her how to bang her highchair tray – a fun game for her to play after a meal while you are clearing up. As she gets the hang of it, you could also get her banging the floor with her spoon or give her a selection of upturned saucepans of different sizes to bang away at – an instant drum kit. Eventually, your baby will cope with two drumsticks – a wooden spoon in each hand – and will have a wonderful time bashing pans.

Benefits

Encourages a sense of rhythm
Babies love rhythm; some research suggests that they are born with it. They are certainly able to bang out a simple rhythm from a very young age. Encouraging your baby to bang 'drums' is a good way to tune into this natural rhythm until she is old enough to stand up and dance.

Improves dexterity
It requires some considerable dexterity to hit a 'drum' with a 'drumstick', especially with a stick in each hand. Doing this will encourage her to use her hands separately, for which she'll need some coordination. You'll also notice that, in time, your baby is able to bang her 'drums' harder and with more vigour – again this requires dexterity and will help refine her hand–eye coordination. She'll be motivated to perfect this skill because the better she is, the louder the noise she makes.

Demonstrates cause and effect
As your baby learns that she has an impact on the world – if she bangs something it makes a noise – she'll grow in confidence and discover how she can control her surroundings.

Promotes having fun
Your baby will love making a big noise, either by bashing her highchair or using wooden spoons to bang saucepans. She'll find the racket she makes exciting, stimulating and possibly very funny.

40 Hide the Toy

From about eight months, babies start to look for toys that they happen to drop or lose. By now, they have passed the object-permanence milestone and so no longer assume that when something is out of sight it means it doesn't exist. So, if a small car rolls under the sofa your baby may well search for it, especially if it's still partly visible. This new skill gives you scope to have lots of fun hiding things. Try putting a small car in a tube (for instance, an empty kitchen roll) and let your baby look for it. She'll have to tip the tube up to get it out, or peep through one end to be able to see it. Do give her lots of help so that she doesn't become confused.

What you need

Any of the following:

- Small toys
- Empty kitchen roll
- Clock with a loud tick
- Musical box
- Blanket
- Cushion
- Tea towel

You can also play 'hunt the ticking clock'. Put a clock under a cushion and let your baby work out which cushion it's under. Two cushions is ample choice at this age. Or hide a musical box: wind it up, then put it somewhere easy to find and encourage her to crawl towards the sound.

Make sure the things you hide aren't completely out of sight: with the clock under the cushion, if the clock is big the cushion will be higher than the other cushion; the music box could stick a little way out from under the blanket. Alternatively, let your baby see you hiding things. At this age, she needs lots of very obvious clues because, until she is one year old, if she can't see the object at all she won't look for it.

Benefits

Teaches how to locate sound

As your baby's hearing develops, she will get better at working out where sounds are coming from. Searching for a ticking clock or a musical box will give her practice at locating sounds and this will help to develop her sense of sound direction. This is part of her auditory processing development, which is the way babies understand and interpret the sounds they hear. It is one thing for the ear to be able to pick up a noise, but the brain then needs to ascertain what the sound is, where it is coming from and how to react to it.

Improves dexterity

Tipping up tubes, lifting cushions and searching underneath blankets will all help your baby to practise her fine motor skills.

Encourages curiosity

Hunting for toys and other objects will encourage your baby to be curious and to search for answers. Being inquisitive will be an essential part of her learning throughout her life. If, at this young age, your baby learns that searching enables her to find what she's looking for, it will help her to be more confident in her quest for knowledge in years to come.

41 Family Photos

It can be fun to sit down with your baby and look at a family photo album. Just as you would with a story book, point to the people in the photos and talk about what they are doing. The more familiar they are to your baby the better – photos of your baby with close relatives are ideal. You could also watch family videos together – again, keep to close family as this will be most interesting to your baby at this age.

What you need

- A family photo album
- Home videos

Benefits

Helps improve language

As you talk about the various people, your baby will learn to understand new words and extend his listening vocabulary.

Promotes understanding of the world

Your baby will start to learn that the people he sees in photos are different to those he sees in real life. This will help teach him about the concept of pictures and photography. Likewise, watching a family video will help him start to understand about film.

OLDER BABY

42 Outside Play

Once your baby is on the move, you can let her crawl outside through grass and encourage her to inspect insects, worms and snails. Tell her what these creatures are called and try to explain what they are doing – some ants may be trying to move a leaf, a snail might be hiding in its shell and a worm might be busy digging itself into the ground where it's nice and cool out of the sun. Show your baby how a ladybird can crawl over your hand, then ask her if she'd like to have a go, but don't force her if she's reluctant.

What you need

- Garden or park

Benefits

Gives an introduction to nature
Showing garden creatures to your baby from an early age will encourage her to be both aware of and interested in nature. Being interested in a subject is an important part of learning, so this will help her in years to come.

Provides a sensory experience
Crawling through grass, feeling a cool worm on her skin and the tickle of a beetle across her palm are all sensory experiences that may be new to your baby.

43 Bath-time Fun

Bath time is a wonderful play opportunity and there's a lot to be learnt from playing with water. Water play really comes into its own once your baby is able to sit up in the bath as this allows him to really experiment with his bath toys.

At this age your baby won't need much in the way of bath toys and will be content with something as simple as a plastic duck; show him how to push it along through the water, push it into the side of the bath and push it under the water. Any bath toy will do, and if you haven't got any then improvise. Just choose things that can't be damaged by water, aren't sharp or dangerous and can float. You can use everyday objects, for example a plastic cup. And, if your baby has any non-bath toys that happen to be plastic and float, you can pop those in the bath for him to play with.

What you need

Any of the following:

- Toys that float
- Sponge
- Something to pour water from
- Plastic zip-up sandwich bag

Pouring is also fun in the bath and a free-flow beaker can be used to make a fountain. Toy watering cans work well too and there are also bath toys available that are designed for this purpose. Fill up your container with fairly warm water before bath time; use drinking water if possible because your baby is quite likely to drink some, and use warm water so that it's not too much of a shock if he pours the water on himself. You too can pour water onto your baby: over his legs and, as he becomes more confident, over his head to pretend it's raining.

You could also give your baby a sponge to play with. He's bound to suck it, so keep it clean and replace it regularly. It's also worth ensuring your baby isn't

thirsty before bath time as this will reduce his urge to drink the bath water. Show him how you can squeeze the water out of the sponge and then dunk it in the bath to absorb water once again.

You can also make a wonderful bath toy simply by half-filling a plastic zip-up sandwich bag with water and putting a plastic toy inside. Your baby will have fun squeezing the toy and the water in the bag.

Benefits

Introduces scientific concepts

Seeing things float in the bath, pouring water and squeezing the water-filled sandwich bag will all teach your baby about the properties of water. The sponge will demonstrate how heavy water is. Simply playing in the bath will familiarize your baby with water and so increase his understanding of it.

Builds water confidence

The more fun your baby has in the bath the better. Don't worry if his face and head get wet because a boisterous bath time will help boost his confidence in water. Dads often excel at bath-time games because not only do they tend to splash more than moms, they are also less likely to notice water going everywhere and so remain nice and relaxed. This is one of the best ways of teaching your baby to love water.

44 Animal Talk

Babies are able to imitate animal sounds – and other sounds, for that matter – before they can form actual words. Some babies start making noises from around eight months and most are keen to imitate all kinds of sounds by around eleven months.

Encourage your baby to make different noises by having some animal fun time. Gather together a collection of her soft toys – choose a variety of animals that make sounds, such as tigers, lions, dogs, ducks and cats. Then pick up one of the animals and make the appropriate noise: 'rrrrroaw' says the lion, or 'woof woof' says the dog. Don't put pressure on your baby to make a noise back – it will take a little while before she is able to do that.

What you need

- Cuddly or plastic toy animals

Simply show her the animal and make the noise. You could also pretend to be the animal yourself, perhaps by getting onto all fours and imitating its sound. Your baby will love you doing this and will probably want to join in. Keep saying the name of the animal you are imitating, and you could put the toy version on the floor to join in too.

Whenever you see real animals, take a bit of time to point them out to your baby, especially if they are making a noise; if a dog is barking, stop and listen with your child and explain that the dog is making a noise, perhaps saying 'hello'. Then imitate the dog's woofing noise. This will encourage your child to try to make the sound too. If you're reading together and come across pictures of animals, talk about the sounds that the animals make.

You could also use plastic animals to teach your child about the sounds – you can buy sets of farm or zoo animals. Use these to make up a simple story for your baby, making sure you incorporate the appropriate animal noises, of course. Give her the animals to hold and try asking her, 'What does the chicken say?' Eventually she'll start making the sounds herself, at which point give her lots of praise. If she doesn't seem keen to make the sounds just yet, don't pressurize her, just do it yourself.

Don't stop at animal noises: point out car indicators, helicopters, anything that makes a sound, and demonstrate the noises. Once your baby starts to copy sounds there will be no stopping her. Some babies can imitate all kinds of noises, such as seagulls, sirens and car engines, well before they are able to talk.

Benefits

Helps with language development
Mimicking sounds is essential to learning to talk and your baby will learn to use her mouth and tongue in new ways so that she can form various sounds. For example, the 'brrrm' sound for a car requires her to make a noise using the front of her mouth, and the 'woof' sound of a dog encourages her to move her lips forward.

Encourages listening
Imitating noises requires good listening skills, and your baby will have to listen carefully to each sound before she is able to make it herself.

45 Box of Bits

From about nine months, babies love putting things into boxes and taking them out again. Give your baby his own box and fill it with a variety of household objects that are safe for him to put in his mouth – babies of this age love to explore with their mouths, which are more sensitive than their fingers, as their fine motor skills still aren't very developed. Get your baby's box out for special play sessions. He shouldn't have access to it all the time as it won't seem so special. Also, his memory still won't be very good so he will probably think it's something he hasn't seen before each time you get it out.

What you need

- Medium-size cardboard box (you could cover it to make it look nice if you wish)

Any of the following:

- Sieve
- Colander
- Wooden spoon
- Pair of socks
- Hat
- Magazine
- Plastic toys
- Tea towel
- Teaspoon

Talk about all the different things in the box but let your baby lead the exploration, and leave it to him to set the pace and decide which object he's going to pull out or put in next. For added interest you could try wrapping up one of the objects in coloured tissue paper for your baby to unwrap. You don't have to help your baby to explore his box of bits all the time; it's fine to let him play on his own.

Benefits

Boosts language development

As you and your baby explore the box of bits, he will hear you say the names of the various objects and this will enhance his understanding. He'll be expanding his listening vocabulary for when he is ready to start talking in a few months' time.

Improves dexterity

It requires skill for your baby to guide objects in and out of containers; he'll need both his fine motor skills and hand–eye coordination. As well as picking the objects up, he'll also be putting them down and this means he'll be letting go of them for a purpose rather than because he can. Each time he puts something in the box, he'll be making a conscious decision to let the object go and also where to put it. Putting things into containers is the first step to mastering a shape sorter, which your baby will no doubt play with when he's a bit older.

Encourages an enquiring mind

Encouraging your baby to explore and investigate the world will help him to develop his sense of curiosity. Wanting to understand more about his environment is an essential part of learning.

Increases independence

Once your baby is sitting unsupported he'll be able to play with his box of bits by himself. It's important that babies learn to play by themselves as this will help them to become more self-reliant in the future. Just a few minutes of solo play is plenty at this stage, and do be aware that your baby may become tired from sitting if it's a new skill.

46 Animal Fun

The sooner your baby gets used to domestic animals the better. If she is familiar with pets before about eighteen months, this will be a big advantage as this is the age that fear usually sets in; babies tend not to get frightened until then. If you've got your own cat or dog, this makes things easier. Cats tend to be less available for playing with babies than dogs – they run off – so she may have to make do with waving at the cat in the garden or perhaps seeing it when it's eating. Occasionally your cat may be asleep somewhere at home, in which case you could help your baby to stroke it.

If you're a cat owner, you'll know the signs that the cat may be about to scratch and it is therefore wise to keep your baby away. When the cat is relaxed, your baby will probably enjoy the feel of the cat's fur and its warmth. Keep this encounter short – remember that you are also training the cat to

What you need

- Child-friendly cats and dogs

Benefits

Encourages a love of animals

If you teach your baby to feel confident around animals, he will be able to enjoy them rather than fearing them. As a child, he will no doubt come into contact with animals from time to time and it is much better that this is a positive experience rather than a frightening one.

Improves coordination

Stroking a cat or dog gently requires some coordination – if your baby gets it wrong the animal will run away.

Helps develop self-control

Cats won't give babies a second chance: if your baby is noisy, chases the cat or pulls its tail it will run away, so he'll have to learn self-control if he wants the cat to stick around.

Encourages friendship

Babies quickly form relationships with pets, particularly dogs, who will tolerate them more than cats. It can be very rewarding for your baby to get to know a dog well and feel confident playing with it.

get used to your baby and you don't want to put it off.

If your little one is crawling, you can teach her to sit down near the cat and not to shout or cry when she sees it so that it is less likely to run away – when the cat does escape, explain that it will come back later. You could encourage your baby to wave hello to cats and dogs when she's out in the buggy.

When approaching a dog, always do so from the head end and put out a closed fist – you can show your baby how to do this. Always check with the owner before going near a dog. Once it has smelt you and your baby, you can show him how to gently stroke and pat the dog. If he gets to know a dog well – yours or a friend's – you can let him crawl after it, and perhaps hold its lead from his buggy (even once he's walking it will be a long time before he's able to keep up with the dog).

Safety first

Always wash your baby's hands after she has touched an animal.

47 Drop and Crash

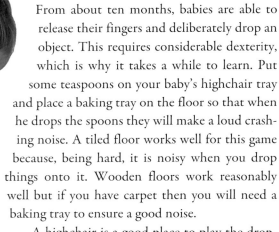

From about ten months, babies are able to release their fingers and deliberately drop an object. This requires considerable dexterity, which is why it takes a while to learn. Put some teaspoons on your baby's highchair tray and place a baking tray on the floor so that when he drops the spoons they will make a loud crashing noise. A tiled floor works well for this game because, being hard, it is noisy when you drop things onto it. Wooden floors work reasonably well but if you have carpet then you will need a baking tray to ensure a good noise.

A highchair is a good place to play the dropping game, simply because your baby will be high up so the crashes will be nice and loud when he

What you need

- A highchair
- A baking tray (if you have carpeted floors)

Any of the following:

- Teaspoons
- Plastic cups and plates
- Scrunched-up newspaper ball

drops things! If you don't have a highchair, sit your baby on your knee at a table and let him pick up objects from the table to drop on the floor.

This game has lots of variations. For example, you could put some plastic cups and plates and scrunched-up newspaper balls on your baby's highchair tray so that he can have fun dropping them. It's your job to pick up all the objects and return them to your baby so he can have another go. Giving him lots of things to drop is certainly easier than having to continually pick things up one at a time.

You could also try putting the baking tray inside a cardboard box. Not only will this give your baby some aiming practice; if he's a good aim and manages to get some of the objects into the box, it will again save you some time clearing up at the end of his game!

Benefits

Improves dexterity

Letting go of objects is a useful skill. Once your baby can let go of something precisely, he will start to have fun picking things up and putting them down with deliberation instead of randomly dropping them.

Improves mathematical and scientific understanding

Dropping things from a height will demonstrate the concept of gravity: objects fall downwards; they don't float about or fall upwards. If he's dropping metal spoons and plastic cups, he'll start to understand the difference between heavy and light: the heavy metal spoons will make more of a crash than the lighter plastic spoons. This game will also introduce the idea that different materials have different properties and react in different ways. Plus, the objects make a different noise depending on whether he drops them onto the metal baking tray or onto the floor. To emphasize this difference you could move his highchair onto a carpet: there will be hardly any sound when he misses the metal tray and drops things onto the soft surface.

Demonstrates cause and effect

Picking up an object and dropping it onto a noisy surface encourages your baby to anticipate the result of his action. He'll start to learn that he is making something happen and this will teach him about cause and effect. He'll also work out that, when he drops things, you pick them up. This will give him a sense of control over his world, which he will love.

48 Target Practice

By about eleven months, some babies will be having great fun throwing anything they can get their hands on – food, toys, beakers, and so on. This is a normal developmental stage called casting out and it's one stage on from being able to deliberately let go of objects.

If your baby likes throwing, you can have fun setting up targets for him. A wastepaper basket to throw balls into works well, although he'll need to stand very close to the bin.

Another fun game is throwing small wet sponges at dad's face – it's probably best to play this one outside. You could cut up a large sponge, give your baby a bowl of water, show him what to do and then let the fun begin! Humour develops at around eleven months, too, and your little one will probably find this game hilarious – especially if there's lots of mock coughing and spluttering from dad as he gets wet. If your baby is reasonably confident with water, dad could have a turn at throwing wet sponges at him; of course, he would need to be extremely gentle.

Throwing bread to the ducks is a time-tested throwing game that your

What you need

Any of the following:

- Newspaper
- Wastepaper basket
- Small sponges
- Bowl of water
- Bread
- Two dining chairs
- Bed sheet
- Lightweight balls

Benefits

Improves coordination

Your baby will need reasonable hand–eye coordination to be able to throw at all, and certainly to be able to aim. As he concentrates on throwing towards his target, he'll need to really focus on what he is doing.

Encourages humour

It's a wonderful experience when your baby begins to show humour and is something that should be encouraged. A sense of humour will enable him to laugh when things go wrong – in this case, dad getting wet and, hopefully, him getting wet too. Being able to laugh easily will help him to be more resilient in later life.

baby will probably love. Use bread that isn't too stale because your baby is bound to have a bite himself. Make sure you break it up for him or he's likely to throw a whole slice in at once. The first few times he probably won't be able to concentrate on how to break up the bread because he'll be too excited at watching the ducks, but, with time, he'll enjoy being in charge of his own bread supply.

A good game for a rainy day involves putting a bed sheet over a couple of dining chairs and encouraging your baby to throw things over the top – nothing too heavy or he may do some damage. Lightweight balls work well, or balls of newspaper. The most classic throwing game of all is playing catch with a ball. Your baby is too young to catch a ball himself yet, but he will have fun throwing the ball to you and be thrilled and impressed when you catch it. Use a small, lightweight ball that will be easy for your baby to throw.

49 All Fall Down

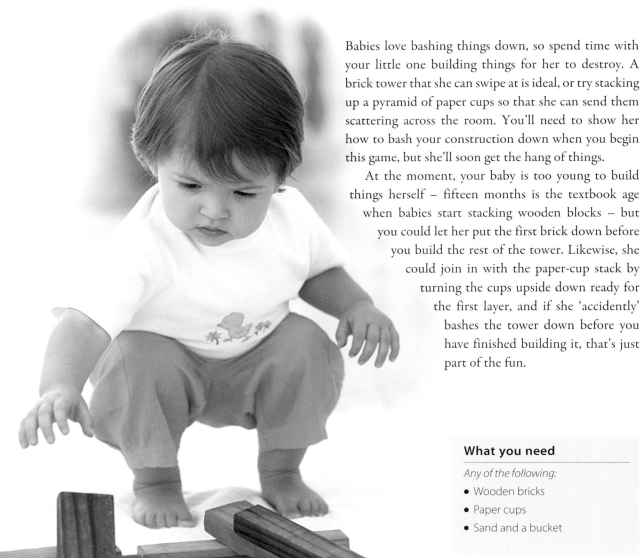

Babies love bashing things down, so spend time with your little one building things for her to destroy. A brick tower that she can swipe at is ideal, or try stacking up a pyramid of paper cups so that she can send them scattering across the room. You'll need to show her how to bash your construction down when you begin this game, but she'll soon get the hang of things.

At the moment, your baby is too young to build things herself – fifteen months is the textbook age when babies start stacking wooden blocks – but you could let her put the first brick down before you build the rest of the tower. Likewise, she could join in with the paper-cup stack by turning the cups upside down ready for the first layer, and if she 'accidently' bashes the tower down before you have finished building it, that's just part of the fun.

What you need

Any of the following:

- Wooden bricks
- Paper cups
- Sand and a bucket

OLDER BABY

Sandcastles are the classic example of building up and bashing down. Your baby can help to fill the bucket with sand, then assist with packing the sand firmly into the bucket with her hands. Once you have turned the bucket over, your baby can pat the top or even give it a good bash with her spade before the exciting moment when you lift off the bucket to reveal the sandcastle.

Because she's still too young to build these structures by herself, this is very much a game that the two of you can play together, which will make it especially good fun.

Benefits

Introduces scientific concepts
Your baby may appear to be playing a simple game of bashing things down, but she's actually exploring the laws of gravity as she watches the various structures crash down. She'll also be learning about different materials – wood, paper and sand – which all have different weights and properties and so require different techniques to form them into structures.

Allows her to control her world
Your baby will find bashing down a structure that you have just created extremely satisfying, especially if it is a particularly tall or elaborate structure. This will give her a sense of control of her world, which she will enjoy because most of the time she has very little say in what goes on. She's still too young for choices and so doesn't get to decide what happens in her life, such as what she wears or eats, and also when she sleeps or goes out. Bashing down a large structure will give her a feeling of power.

Promotes humour
Your baby may well be very amused when she bashes down a sandcastle or a paper-cup tower, especially once she understands the concept of humour. Humour is a very important strategy for coping with life, so do encourage this, perhaps by pretending to cry – in an obvious mock way – when she destroys your stack of bricks.

50 Let's Pretend

As your baby approaches the age of one, he will start to imitate gestures and the use of objects. For example, if he sees you using your mobile phone he may want to copy, so you could give him an old, non-working mobile phone or a toy one. Likewise, you could give him a regular toy telephone so that he can imitate you making a phone call on the landline. You could also give him a toy steering wheel so that he can imitate you driving the car.

Wiping surfaces can be a popular activity around now if this is something that your baby sees you do. If you give your baby his own damp cloth, he'll have a wonderful time wiping his highchair tray.

Keys also fascinate babies, so find some old ones and put them together on a key ring so that they look authentic. He may put them in his pocket just like daddy. Or perhaps he'll see you on your computer; if you've got an old keyboard this would make a lovely toy for your baby to bash away on.

Wherever possible, encourage your baby to imitate what he sees. So, for example, if you have a pet cat and call it in for

What you need

Any of the following:

- Toy telephone
- Old mobile phone
- Cloth for wiping up
- Keys
- Old keyboard

food by shaking a box of cat biscuits, let your baby do the shaking. Or perhaps he sees you shaking out wet laundry; again, give your baby a small item of clothing to shake so that he can join in.

If you wear glasses, your baby will want to wear glasses too – baby sunglasses will do. And if he sees you cleaning your glasses, give him his own cleaning cloth so that he can join in.

Your baby will also imitate your gestures. If you are chatting away to a friend and shaking your head, you may notice that your baby is staring, mesmerized by what he sees and is shaking his head just like you.

The imitation stage can be hilarious, but try to resist the temptation to laugh at your baby as this can be quite discouraging. Instead, involve him whenever you can. If he's mimicking your mannerisms as you chat, you could look at him sincerely and ask, 'Wouldn't you agree?'

Benefits

Teaches new skills

By watching you carefully and then wiping his highchair with a cloth, your baby will improve his dexterity and refine his fine motor skills. He'll also be learning a new skill: imitation. This is a primary way of learning: for example, if you were learning to play tennis, you would imitate how your coach serves and only once you'd accomplished the basic technique would you move on to refine this new skill.

Helps prepare for imaginary play

Imitation is a step towards imaginary play, when children start to look beyond reality in order to play a game: for example, pretending that a wooden block is a tea cup and that they're having a cup of tea. This is an essential stage of development, and preparation for this type of play is very important. At the moment, your baby will simply imitate you as you talk on the telephone, but it won't be long before he is speaking to an imaginary person. Likewise, at the moment he may tap a computer just like daddy, but before long he'll actually *be* the daddy in an imaginary home or office of his own.

Part Three

Toddler
Twelve to Twenty-four Months

Can you believe it? Your tiny baby is a toddler already! So much has changed during the last twelve months, and the year to come is sure to be just as eventful. This chapter is full of ideas to boost your toddler's development and help you to have fun together in the process.

Between the ages of one and two, your toddler will pass some incredible milestones as she learns to walk and talk. She will also start to play in the traditional sense of the word – this is the age when you can bring out the paints, glue, sandpit, toy tool box and tea set. Your toddler will already be able to sit up and play, and she will also be very mobile – either crawling at speed or up on her feet and toddling. She may also be able to say a word or two. But, whatever stage your toddler has reached, there's no doubt that she will make amazing progress during the next year.

Learning through play

Children reach the various milestones at their own pace and in their own time, but if you set up lots of games that encourage your toddler to learn, and present an environment that will encourage her physical, mental and social development, you will almost certainly bring forward these milestones to some extent.

Although you can't teach your toddler by giving her lessons or training sessions, there's plenty you can do through play. The aim of this book isn't to educate your child, but to give her creative playful activities that make her eager for knowledge and also to prepare her for school and learning as she gets older.

Time to talk

As well as helping your toddler's mental and physical development, we've also included lots of activities that can help with speech and language. Vocabulary is a crucial learning tool, and the more words your child knows, the more she will expand her knowledge and understanding of the world. Enjoying interesting activities with your child is a wonderful way to help her with her vocabulary, both learning to say the words and learning to understand them. Speech also requires good control of the lips, tongue and soft palate, which is why we have included play ideas to develop these.

Getting messy

From about one year, your child will be old enough to enjoy playing with paint, play-dough, sand, water and glue. Messy play offers countless benefits, from the obvious creative development and dexterity, to the less obvious sensory development. It's crucial that your child spends time doing messy play because getting used to handling different textures will avoid sensory problems later on: children who are kept very clean can start to feel upset whenever they get messy or dirty. Interestingly, children having play therapy are always asked to wear old clothes because they are encouraged to do lots of messy play.

Have fun together

Your toddler will be enormous fun to play with in the coming year, especially as she now has a sense of humour. What's more, her favourite playmates in the world will be mom, dad and other close carers who she knows well and loves. She still prefers you to other children her own age because she's simply too young to engage in social, interactive play. Because stranger-phobia kicks in at this age, peaking at about fifteen months, she will feel much happier playing with adults she knows well rather than those she isn't so sure of. This means that playing with your toddler will not only give her entertainment, but comfort too, so make the most of your adoring little playmate, get down on the floor and get messy.

51 Sand Play

You may have wonderful childhood memories of hours spent playing on the beach. Now your one-year-old can start to enjoy sand too, either at a beach or in a sandpit. If you have a garden you can set up a sandpit at home, otherwise you may find one at a local park or playgroup.

Because your toddler is still very young, you'll need to spend a little time showing him how to play. You could smooth some sand into a road for a digger to drive along, and perhaps build a tunnel for it to go through. Or add water to some sand, then use plastic dishes or a bucket to make sand cakes – twigs make good birthday candles.

Sand can also be very therapeutic and has been used by psychologists for over seventy years to help children express their feelings through play. In this process, known as sandplay (or sandtray) therapy, the child is

What you need

- Sand or a sandpit

Any of the following:

- Plastic dishes
- Bucket and spade
- Toy people
- Toy animals
- Toy vehicles

given what he needs to make a miniature world in his sandpit: for example, toy people, animals, cars, diggers, houses and shops (you can make toy buildings out of cereal boxes or shoe boxes). The important thing with sandplay therapy is to be able to play with your child in a non-authoritative way. Let him lead the play; this can actually be quite difficult because you'll be tempted to instruct and suggest ideas, but it's important to react and respond to what your child wants to do. This style of play doesn't have to be limited to sand; try to allow your toddler to lead the play for at least a few minutes each day, whatever he is playing with.

Benefits

Teaches scientific principles

Your child will learn about the properties of sand: what it feels like, what it can do, how warm or cold it is and how its texture changes when you add water.

Boosts sensory development

Touching the sand and getting messy will help your toddler to feel comfortable with different textures as he gets older, and not get upset if he happens to get dirty.

Provides anxiety relief

Sand has an inexplicable soothing effect. Just the sensory experience of walking on a beach and having sand between your toes can be soothing. Likewise, children seem to find handling sand pleasurable and calming. Setting up a sand-therapy session for your child can help him cope with his emotions and feel more relaxed, even from a very young age. Just as adults can find relief in seeing a counsellor who listens intently to everything they say, toddlers can feel 'listened to' if they are allowed to be in charge as they play with an adult. This is different from simply playing on their own, because everything they do is being observed and approved of by an attentive grown-up.

As your child's speech develops, he may occasionally re-create a difficult event in his sandpit such as falling over or being frightened by a dog. Resist the temptation to ask questions which demand a response and put pressure on your child. Instead, simply comment: for example, 'Goodness, the little boy must have been frightened by the dog.' This puts no pressure on him but will hopefully encourage him to continue talking and reap some therapeutic benefit from his sand world. Of course, if there is a serious issue that needs to be dealt with you must seek professional help.

52 Blowing Bubbles

What you need

- A pot of bubble mixture and a blower which you can buy from toy shops, newsagents and supermarkets.

How to make your own

Mix a mug of water with two tablespoons of concentrated washing-up liquid. To make the bubbles strong and long lasting, try adding a teaspoon of glycerine (available from chemists). Add another half-teaspoon of glycerine for giant bubbles. For best results, leave the bubble mixture overnight to give it a chance to settle after it has been mixed. Keep it covered to avoid the water evaporating. You can use a straw as a blower or make one out of garden wire or, for giant bubbles, a wire coat hanger.

You can blow lots of little bubbles using a straw, or larger bubbles using a blower. The slower and more steadily you blow, the bigger the bubble. When it's your child's turn to blow, teach her to blow slowly and help her to hold the blower steadily.

Benefits

Helps develop muscle control for speech

Blowing bubbles helps to control the lips and will teach your child how to move her lips forward. We move our lips forward into a bubble-blowing shape during speech when we make the sounds 'w', 'sh' and 'oo', and for this reason speech therapists often use bubbles to help children who are having difficulty making these sounds.

Your child will probably blow very hard at first but to blow a successful bubble you need to blow gently, and this requires more muscle control and helps develop oral motor functioning. Blowing giant bubbles using a rounded coat hanger requires particularly good muscle control.

Increases vocabulary

Bubbles can help to teach a child different body parts. For example, a bubble may pop on her head, foot, elbow, arm and so on. If your child wants to catch a bubble, wet her hands because bubbles are less likely to pop on wet surfaces than on dry ones.

Assists mathematical development

You can count the bubbles and talk about high bubbles, low bubbles, big bubbles, small bubbles and bubbles descending. This is a fun introduction to mathematical and scientific concepts including gravity (bubbles coming down), comparing object sizes (big and small bubbles), and the position of objects (high and low).

Produces a calming effect

Blowing bubbles can quickly soothe a toddler who is having a tantrum. When your child sees something different and unusual, it will activate the 'seeking' system in the primitive part of her brain and make her feel curious and interested. Because the seeking system is in the lower brain, it can easily override the brain's rage or distress systems. It also triggers high levels of the nuerotransmitter dopamine, which reduces stress.

Creates humour

If you try to catch a bubble and pretend to be sad when it pops (cue, comedy crying), your toddler will probably find this amusing. This teaches your child to laugh when things don't go as planned, which is good preparation for later in life.

53 Cruising Obstacle Course

What you need

- Sofa or chairs

Any of the following:

- Fruit that doesn't bruise easily
- Small toys

The average age for toddlers to start walking is around fourteen months. However, before your child walks, he will spend time cruising – shuffling around on his feet, often sideways, hanging onto furniture for balance. This is an important stage in preparing to walk and you can encourage your toddler to spend time standing by setting up a cruising obstacle course.

Line up a row of dining chairs – about three will do, but the more the better. If they are heavy chairs they will be nice and stable and you can place them down the centre of a

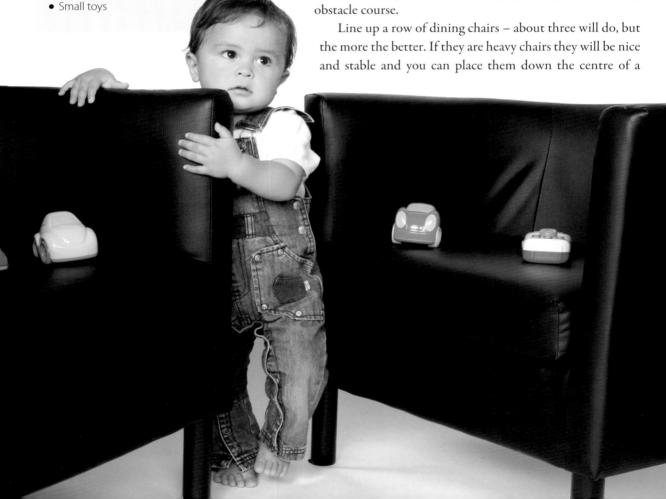

room, otherwise you will need to position the chairs with their backs to a wall. Place some fun objects on the chairs for your toddler to discover, such as toy cars and diggers or any toys on wheels. Stand him up in the middle of the row and let him decide which way he wants to cruise; sometimes children find it easier to cruise in one direction than another, which is why it's good to give him the choice rather than putting him at one end. Eventually he'll be skilled enough to cruise up and down the row of chairs.

A variation of this game is to place fruit along the row of chairs; choose types that aren't easily squashed or bruised such as oranges, lemons and limes. Your child will be drawn to the bright colours. In fact, you can put all kinds of interesting objects along the chairs for your child to find and explore.

Make life easier

You could put toys along a sofa which your child can cruise along. This is quicker to set up than chairs and so less frustrating if your toddler decides that she's not in the mood for this game.

Benefits

Prepares your toddler to walk

Cruising teaches your toddler to balance, and this is an important step in preparing to walk. It also strengthens the hip muscles which support his legs for walking. Your toddler will gain strength and confidence and will eventually be able to let go of the chairs and walk independently, initially taking just a few wobbly steps.

Encourages independence

Setting up a cruising obstacle course encourages your toddler to practise his walking skills independently. An alternative is that you hold his hands from the front and help him to walk, but lots of babies start to expect you to give them walking practice on demand and become irritated if they have to wait. By encouraging independent practise, you will avoid this.

Motivates your baby to explore

If your baby sees an object at one end of his cruising chairs, he may become inquisitive and try to shuffle along them to investigate. This curiosity is a key part of learning about the world.

54 Get Pushy

Before your toddler learns to walk, she'll be able to totter around aided by a push-along toy of some kind. When she is at the cruising stage, you could try giving her a toy of this nature to help her balance. Wooden trolleys with toy blocks in work well because they are quite sturdy and will give good support. This kind of toy often makes a good first-birthday present as, at this age, lots of children are standing and possibly cruising, but not yet walking. Once your toddler has taken her first steps and is able to walk without support, she'll continue to enjoy her push-along trolley or truck

What you need

Any of the following:
- Wooden trolley (with toy blocks)
- Push-along walker or truck
- Toy buggy
- Your toddler's buggy

What's in a colour?

Although lots of toy buggies are pink and targeted at girls, little boys enjoy them too. Blue ones are available, although you may have to search a bit harder. But if you can only get pink, you'll find that your son doesn't mind in the slightest until he is at least three years old and starts to become socially aware.

but will use it in a different way. Encourage her to put her favourite toys in it to push around.

When she's really steady on her feet, she may enjoy a toy buggy. These tend to be very light and don't give much support to toddlers who aren't yet walking reasonably confidently, although you can load them up with books or wooden blocks to make them heavier and more stable. Once your toddler is ready for a buggy, she will have tremendous fun pushing her favourite toys around. She'll also enjoy taking her buggy outside, perhaps pushing teddy around the block, or you could take it to the park for her to play with. As your toddler approaches two, you could give her a little bag to hang on the handle bars so that she can carry more possessions.

An alternative to pushing a toy buggy around is to let your toddler push her own buggy. You will need to stand behind her to steer and discreetly help her to push. Again, she may like to take a favourite teddy, toy or other treasured object to push in her buggy.

Benefits

Provides walking practice

Pushing a trolley helps your toddler to get into a forward-leaning posture. This is a very natural stance in the early stages when toddlers stand and walk a little bit like apes. Parents often hold their toddler's hands up behind their heads for balance. This forces the child to lean backwards slightly, which is a very unstable position.

Boosts fitness

When toddlers first learn to walk, they become tired quite easily and will often rather stay in their buggy than use their legs. Taking a toy buggy out with you will help to motivate her to get out of her own buggy and walk, which will boost her stamina. Gradually, she will become more keen to walk some of the way when you're out and about.

Develops a sense of self

Putting favourite toys in her buggy, or in a little bag on the handle bars, is an important developmental stage and will help your toddler to see herself as a person, separate from anybody else. Being possessive and wanting to keep her own toys away from other children is part of this developmental stage.

55 City on the Floor

Use brightly coloured masking tape to mark out roads. Stick two parallel strips along the floor, scaling your road to fit your toddler's toy cars, trucks and diggers. Show him how to push his vehicles up and down this road. Make a T-junction so that he can choose which direction they go; perhaps put in a shop to the right and a filling station to the left – you could make these out of cereal boxes or shoe boxes. You could also make a railway line; again, you could use two parallel lines, but this time use a different-coloured masking tape. To make tunnels for the cars and trains to drive through, you could stick toilet rolls to the floor on the railway line and roads. Make sure the toys are small enough to fit through easily or your toddler will become frustrated.

Spend time on the floor with your toddler inventing a story: for example, about a little green car that drives down the road, then turns left and goes to the filling station to get some petrol. Stick four pieces of string (about 8 cm [3 in] long) along the inside of the 'filling station' to make a line of petrol pumps. The story can become as elaborate as you want; as your child gets older, he'll appreciate slightly more complicated stories. You can repeat the same story again and again; toddlers tend to find this quite comforting. Encourage your child to 'help' by pushing the car along the road to the garage, filling the car with 'petrol' and so on. If your little one just wants to watch the story, that's fine too.

As your child approaches his second birthday, you could try giving him a selection of different-sized vehicles and asking him which will fit through the tunnel. Then you can say, 'No, that one's too big', 'Oh, that one is small enough – see, it fits', and so on. This will encourage him to work out which vehicles fit through the tunnel. You can talk about a car turning left or right. Although he is too young to distinguish his left from his right, you can familiarize him with the vocabularly.

What you need

- Two rolls of masking tape in different colours
- Empty toilet rolls or kitchen rolls
- Toy cars, diggers and trains
- Cereal boxes and shoe boxes
- String

Making the most of toys

By now, your toddler may well have acquired various toys that could be incorporated into this game, such as little play people, a garage perhaps, or even a railway track. Do use these as it will demonstrate to your child how to mix and match different toys.

Benefits

Soothes

Inventing an imaginary world with your child will activate the seeking system in his brain. This is in the more primitive part of the brain and so useful for over-ruling other responses in this area of the brain such as anger and tantrums. If your toddler is having a bad day with lots of tantrums, playing this imaginary game will be very effective at calming him.

Improves coordination

Sitting on the floor pushing small cars in between two parallel lines and through tunnels requires reasonable dexterity and hand–eye coordination.

Teaches a sense of scale

Small children don't have a sense of scale and will happily attempt to sit on a miniature toy chair – even though it may only be 4 cm high – or try to 'drive' a 6-cm toy tractor. Then they'll be surprised when the toy disappears under their bottom. Demonstrating that only some cars can fit through a tunnel will teach your child about different sizes and scale. Use words like 'big', 'small', 'wide', 'narrow' and so on. It will be some time before your child is able to grasp the concept of scale and size differences, but this will certainly give him a good grounding.

56 Park Play

If your local park has baby swings (the ones with bars around the seat to stop the child falling out), then chances are it will have some other activities for very small children. Although some playgrounds are excellent for toddlers, others seem to be geared more towards older children, so be prepared to search for a suitable playground that you can get to easily. As your child learns to walk and approaches two, you may find yourself spending increasing amounts of time at the park. If you've already taken your toddler on the swings, you'll find that you can now push him higher because his balance is improving, as is his ability to hold on. This means he will also be ready to try other activities.

From the age of one, you can start riding with your toddler on a roundabout – just sit him on your knee. When you get off, hold his hands (if he's walking) and tell him that he'll be feeling dizzy from the roundabout

What you need

- A local play area with activities for toddlers

– he'll love the sensation. By about eighteen months your toddler will be able to sit on the roundabout while you push, keeping one hand on his back. You'll obviously be the best judge as to when he can go on the roundabout without any support at all.

Many playgrounds have small-scale climbing frames that your child can have fun exploring. Some children actually learn to climb before they can walk because it involves the use of both arms and legs. You'll have to watch your child closely if he decides to climb up a slide ladder, to ensure he doesn't fall off, but he'll quickly develop his sense of balance.

Safety first

Up to eighteen months (when children start to show fear), stay very close to your child at the playground. It's believed that up to this age curiosity far outweighs judgement and there is no sense of danger.

Benefits

Improves fitness

Some toddlers don't enjoy walking very much because it wears them out, but in a playground setting these very same toddlers will happily walk from one activity to another without even being aware that they're doing so. They"ll be so absorbed in their surroundings that they won't feel tired until later. All this exercise will strengthen your toddler's larger muscles and gross motor skills, his arms and legs developing as he climbs.

Improves balance

As mentioned in the last section (*see activity 37, Go for a Swing*), the repetitive motion of playing on the swing stimulates the vestibular system. Now your toddler will also improve his balance as he learns to climb a frame and also hang on to a moving roundabout.

Provides an introduction to playground politics

The playground is a good environment for meeting other children. Although your child is still too young to play cooperatively, he'll enjoy watching other children, particularly the slightly older ones. He will also start to witness the hierarchies and pecking order. Learning to step out of the way of older children is a useful skill that will help to keep him safe. We're certainly not suggesting that your child becomes a timid victim, but if he has enough awareness to move out of the way when a boisterous four- or five-year-old comes racing past, he won't accidentally get knocked over.

57 Out and About

Once your child reaches one year, he is old enough to enjoy child-orientated outings such as a zoo or farm – he'll especially like the petting area. And, as he approaches his second birthday, he'll cope well with a puppet show or even a circus. The circus is a particularly fun treat with all the colour and music. What's more, it's noisy so no-one will mind if your toddler shouts or makes a fuss, and there are constant scene changes to hold his attention.

What you need

- Information about what's on in your area (from a local newspaper or a website)

Benefits

Boosts concentration
Having to sit still for a puppet show or to watch a circus will require your toddler to be focused and to concentrate. Even sitting still for as little as 20 minutes is an achievement at this age.

Helps create happy memories
If your toddler does something very different to his everyday life, he may remember it long after the event. This not only helps to develop his long-term memory, but also gives him happy childhood memories that he will keep for life.

Safety first
Always wash your child's hands after touching animals.

TODDLER

58 Pasta Jewellery

Help your toddler to thread dried pasta shapes (such as penne) onto a piece of string to make a bracelet. Leave a space on the string about the length of a piece of pasta, because when you cook it the pasta will expand. You'll need to try the bracelet on your child's wrist to get the size correct. Then cook the bracelet in boiling water and, when the pasta has cooled, let your child wear it – and eat it.

What you need

- Pasta shapes – any with holes in
- String

Benefits

Teaches sense of scale

As you try the pasta on your child's wrist and either add a piece or take one away, she will start to understand about measurements and scale.

Promotes healthy eating

Pasta is a sugar-free snack that your toddler can nibble on between meals.

Try this

Your toddler could paint the bracelet to make it look pretty, in which case don't cook it or let her eat it.

59 Cardboard Fun

There is infinite scope for using cardboard boxes to make playtime more interesting. In just a few minutes a plain old box can become a house, a boat, a car or even a rocket. So if you happen upon a large box, put it aside for your toddler. Or, if you want to get hold of one especially, they are often available for free in supermarkets and some other shops.

The key is to help your child to see the box as something different. To make a car, you could use a marker pen to draw on wheels, then get your child to sit in the box and hand him a paper plate to use as a steering wheel. You could even add an empty toilet roll to the back to make an

What you need

- Cardboard boxes
- Marker pen
- Masking tape
- Paper (or plastic) plate
- Empy toilet roll
- Sharp knife

Benefits

Improves motor skills
Climbing through, in and out of boxes develops the gross motor skills as your toddler will be using his arms and legs.

Promotes imaginative play
We've all heard grandmothers say things like, 'My kids just had a cardboard box and a wooden spoon to play with,' as they look on disapprovingly at today's children playing with elaborate plastic toys. Well, it turns out that they may have a point. Although there's nothing much wrong with fancy plastic toys, the advantage of simple things like cardboard boxes is that they get the imagination going. Your toddler will have to think in order to imagine that a cardboard box is actually a pirate ship or a space rocket. And, the more your child thinks,

the more his brain will develop – just as the more he uses his legs, the more his leg muscles will develop.

Helps develop language
Even if your toddler isn't yet speaking, from the age of one, lots of children are able to imitate noises. Your child is likely to have great fun making car or rocket noises, which can help language development. When it comes to learning to talk, it's essential that parents respond to their child's attempts at speech. If your child hasn't yet started to try saying words, perhaps he will have a go at making car noises. If you respond, 'Wow, that sounds like a fast car; what a noisy engine,' this will encourage him to make more sounds and noises, and eventually have a go at saying a few words.

exhaust pipe. Be as creative as you like. Alternatively, you could leave the box exactly as it is but, once your child is sitting inside it, make car noises as you push it along, or rock the box so that it becomes a boat. Tall, thin boxes make the best rockets; your job is to make it 'blast off'. Encourage your toddler to take his teddy or other favourite toy for a ride in his cardboard vehicle, or push it around in the car, boat or rocket. Whatever the vehicle, your child will probably enjoy making engine noises with you.

If you've got lots of boxes of a similar size you could make a tunnel to crawl through. Stick the boxes together to hold them in place, or stick each one to the floor.

To make a house, you need a really large box, then cut out a door and a window or two using a sharp knife (if you leave one side intact the windows and doors will open and shut). When your child is inside his house, knock on the door and wave through the window.

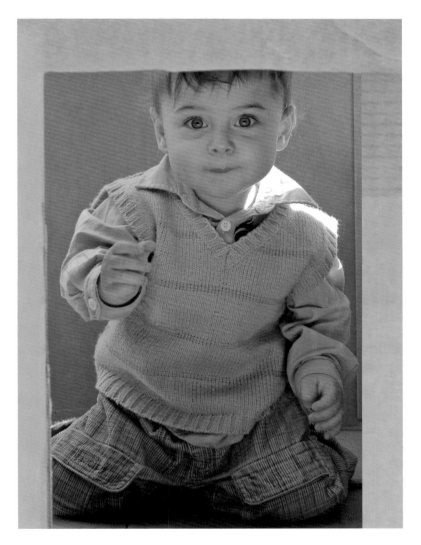

60 Splish Splash Splosh!

Playing with water is a wonderful activity for children, and it doesn't have to be limited to bath time. Once your toddler is steady on her feet, she can stand on a step stool and play at a sink. However, the easiest way is to set up a water-play area outside. If you've got a garden or outside space – no matter how small – you can use either a washing-up bowl full of water, which your child can sit beside or even get into on hot days, or a paddling pool. Give her lots of plastic containers of different colours and sizes and show her how to fill and empty them with water, and how they float when empty and sink when full of water.

You could also give your toddler a plastic jug or toy teapot and show her how to fill it and pour. Plastic washing-powder scoops are also fun because toddlers can 'spoon' water from one container to another. Or you could give her some small plastic toys that will sink in water – plastic farm animals or toy people, perhaps.

What you need

Indoors:

- Sink or bath
- Step stool

Outdoors:

- Washing-up bowl or paddling pool

Any of the following:

- Plastic tea set
- Plastic cups
- Plastic jug
- Plastic washing-powder scoop
- Small plastic toys that will sink in water
- Plastic apron (optional)

Helpful hint

*If you give your child a drink before you start water play,
she's less likely to try to drink the paddling-pool water.*

Benefits

Introduces mathematical concepts

By filling up different-sized containers, your child will discover that small cups overflow easily, and that it's difficult to fill up a big container using a small cup – the basic principles of volume. She'll also discover that large containers of water are heavier than smaller containers. Your toddler won't be analysing this information, or understanding the science. She will simply come to expect large containers of water to be heavier than smaller ones, and having this expectation will eventually help her to understand why objects have different weights.

Teaches about properties of water

As we said in activity 43, Bath-time Fun, playing with water will help to teach your toddler about its properties. She'll see how liquid can be poured, how some objects float on the surface and others sink, how a container may float when it's empty, but if you fill it with water it will sink, and how water makes you wet. Your child is more likely to notice the feeling of being wet if she's wearing dry clothes when she plays with water than if she's placed in the bath naked – her sleeves may be wet for some time afterwards (you can point this out to her).

Boosts water confidence

It is very important for children to become confident around water and the more exposure your child has, the more relaxed she will be. She'll come to see water as fun and won't mind getting wet.

61 Magnetic Families

Once your toddler is standing, he will have great fun playing with fridge magnets stuck to the side of the fridge, washing machine or any other easily accessible metal surface. He'll particularly enjoy pulling the magnets down. So, why not customize your own fridge magnets and have family members stuck to the fridge for your toddler to find? You can buy magnetic picture frames online or from photo shops.

Sit down with your toddler and let him choose some photos to go in the frames; perhaps mommy, daddy, grandparents, pets and, of course, one of himself (you could include a baby picture of him too). When you've finished, he can stick the photos to the fridge and you can have fun talking about the different people. Take time to explain that he used to be a baby but now he has grown into a little boy, and use his baby photo to illustrate how different he is now.

You can teach your child to play with the fridge-magnet characters in a similar way to his toy figures, moving the characters around and making them 'talk'. Playing with the magnets will be particularly good fun because he'll know all the characters. Before long your child will be moving his family characters around the fridge and making them chatter away to each other.

You can even use the magnets to help explain to your child what is going on in his life. For example, when grandparents are planning a visit you can move their photos beside the one of your child and make them say 'hello'. Then, when they've gone home, move the photos away again. Likewise, if you're going to work you can get your photo to say 'goodbye' to your child's picture, then move it away. Of course, do show the photo returning home again.

If you ever have another baby, you can put a picture of your new arrival into a fridge magnet for your older child, or children, to play with.

What you need

- Magnetic photo frames
- Selection of family photos

Digital photos

Digital photos can be printed directly onto fridge magnets (look online or visit a photo shop). These magnets will look better than what you could achieve by simply inserting a printed photo into a frame but will be more expensive. If you have a particularly good photo of your toddler, this will make a lovely gift for family members.

TODDLER

Benefits

Improves dexterity

Moving a fridge magnet around on a metal surface, as well as pulling it off and putting it back on again, requires a gentle touch and will help to develop your child's fine motor skills.

Improves understanding of the world

The photo family is a fun way to teach your toddler about who is in his own family, and the rhythm of everyone coming in and out of his life as grandparents visit and parents leave for work, and so on. It's also a wonderful way to teach him about any new siblings that may arrive on the scene.

62 At One with Nature

We covered outside play in Part Two (activity 42, Outside Play) when your child would probably have been crawling, but once she is walking there is a lot more scope for playing in the garden. Firstly, you can water the plants together. It is useful if your toddler has her own tiny watering can because she'll be too small to lift a normal-sized one. She'll love sprinkling the water over plants and seedlings – particularly if she's planted them herself. One of the most satisfying things to grow in a garden is something you can eat. Your toddler could help you to plant some mixed lettuce-leaf seeds, then water them with you. They grow particularly well in a plant pot and will start to appear within about ten days – your

What you need

- Garden

Any of the following:

- Toy watering can
- Lettuce seeds
- Pots of herbs
- Flower pot
- Hose pipe and sprinkler
- Plastic figures

Gardening without a garden

If you haven't got a garden, you can grow seeds indoors. Cress is a classic: put the seeds on a damp piece of kitchen paper on a saucer. Or you could put a container by your front door, and you and your toddler could plant vegetables and herbs in it – there's no rule that says you must grow flowers at the front of the house.

toddler can keep watering them as they grow. Eventually she can help pick, wash and eat the lettuce. If you happen to be a keen gardener, you can have fun growing all kinds of vegetables with your toddler; potatoes, tomatoes and beans are all reasonably straightforward. Herbs are also very easy to grow and your toddler can help to pick handfuls of herbs to add to the dinner.

You can also use a watering can in other ways. Get out some plastic toy figures and have fun making it rain over them. Show your toddler how they can take shelter from the rain, perhaps inside a flower pot.

On hot days, your toddler can help water the garden with a hose. A hand-held sprinkler can be fun, or if you've got a sprinkler system that moves by itself your toddler will enjoy creeping up to it. There are bound to be some muddy patches where you have over-watered, so you could let your toddler splash about and play in the mud if she wants to!

Benefits

Encourages healthy eating
Fussy eating is particularly common between the ages of one and two years, and vegetables can be especially challenging. Getting your toddler involved in growing vegetables is an effective way to encourage her to eat them.

Promotes muscle development
Carrying a full watering can (even a small one) requires quite a lot of upper-body muscle strength and also a good sense of balance.

Boosts sensory development
Getting splashed by the watering can or from not having much control over the hose will expose your toddler to the sensation of getting wet unexpectedly. This is different from simply getting into the bath where things are more controlled and expected. Getting muddy also gives your child a different sensory experience. Occasionally children develop sensory problems, where they get upset whenever they become messy or dirty. If you remain relaxed about your toddler getting wet and muddy in the garden she will learn to be comfortable with mess, and this should discourage such problems.

Uses the imagination
Making it rain over toy figures will trigger your child's imagination and encourage her to visualize an imaginary world. Using the imagination is very good for brain development.

63 Gingerbread Friends

This is a basic biscuit mix that you can roll out and cut into all kinds of shapes. Flour your child's highchair tray and give him his own ball of pastry to mould and play with. From about fifteen months he'll be able to have a go at rolling it and putting the eyes (raisins) onto the gingerbread men that you have cut out and arranged on the baking tray. Children of this age are often also particularly fascinated with eyes. You can make mouths and noses from small pieces of glacé cherry which your child can stick on. You can also show him where to place the gingerbread man's buttons (more raisins). Of course, you can have fun experimenting with different ingredients for the face and buttons. Do make a point of baking some of your child's creations, however abstract, because he'll be especially proud of them.

When it comes to eating the gingerbread characters, chat to your toddler about how he can bite off the arms, legs or head.

See activity 64, Bake a Cake, for more ideas on how to get your child involved.

What you need

- Small rolling pin
- Gingerbread-man cutter
- Baking tray, lined with greaseproof paper
- 180 g (6½ oz) plain flour
- 125 g (4½ oz) butter, softened
- 60 g (2 oz) caster sugar
- 2 teaspoons ground ginger
- 1 egg yolk (from a small egg), beaten
- raisins
- glacé cherries

How to make gingerbread

Sieve the flour into a mixing bowl and rub in the butter until it resembles fine breadcrumbs. Mix in the sugar and gradually add the egg yolk until the mixture forms a ball. Turn onto a floured surface, roll it out and cut into shapes. Lay them on the baking tray and bake in an oven preheated to 190°C/375°F/Gas 5 for 10–15 minutes.

Benefits

Teaches about body parts

This is a fun way for your child to learn the names of body parts. Because of the simple shape of the gingerbread men, it will be limited to arms, legs, head and, perhaps, eyes. However, every bit of reinforcement helps when it comes to learning and increasing your child's vocabulary.

Helps language development

Baking teaches children lots of words, such as the names of the ingredients and cookery terms like 'weighing', 'mixing', 'baking tray', 'oven' and so on.

Improves dexterity

Putting raisin eyes in place requires your child to use the pincer grip – with his thumb and forefinger. If your child does pastry cooking frequently, he'll become increasingly skilled and, with time, he'll learn to knead and roll the pastry into a ball, use a rolling pin and push down a cutter accurately enough to form a neat shape. This requires good fine motor skills and your child will of course need help to begin with, but from the very start he'll watch the process and be involved in certain stages – even if it's just haphazardly putting the eyes on.

Teaches about spatial awareness and planning

Eventually your child will start to work out how to cut the maximum number of shapes from his rolled-out pastry.

No cookie cutters?

An up-turned beaker can be used instead of a cookie cutter to cut out circles to make faces.

64 Bake a Cake

Children love baking and there are plenty of ways for them to help, from as young as fifteen months. Put your toddler in her highchair so that she can see what's happening, then let her get involved wherever possible. Make sure you wash both your hands and your child's hands before you start.

Show your child how to measure the butter. Explain how the scales work and put them on her highchair tray so that she can touch them. Let her pick up the butter and put it into the mixing bowl. Then measure out the sugar and let your toddler help to pour it into the bowl and beat the sugar and butter together. Take turns with this to get the job done. Let your child touch the eggs before you crack them into the bowl. Again, take

What you need

- Cake tin, greased, or 12 baking cases
- 100 g (4 oz) butter, softened, plus extra for greasing
- 100 g (4 oz) caster sugar
- 2 eggs
- 100 g (4 oz) self-raising flour
- 1 tsp baking powder

Benefits

Improves understanding of the world
Your child will see how mixing up the cake ingredients transforms their consistency, and how putting them in the oven changes them again. She'll also learn about weighing.

Helps speech development
Licking the spoon encourages tongue mobility; this technique is used by speech therapists as, when we speak, the tongue rapidly moves in different directions to produce sounds accurately. Check that your toddler is using her tongue to lick and isn't just sucking the mixture off with her lips. When she has finished licking the spoon, ask her to lick her lips clean, again checking that she uses her tongue.

Helps reduce dribbling
Good tongue control also helps to reduce dribbling. Some children dribble a lot until they're three or four years old, at which point they start to become more socially aware so the dribbling stops. Dribbling is nothing to worry about; it's simply down to excessive saliva production.

Improves manual dexterity
Making a cake involves lots of skills that require your child to be good with her hands: putting butter in the mixing bowl, mixing, spreading the mixture, greasing the tin. If you do some baking together regularly, you'll see your toddler get better and better at these skills.

turns at mixing them in. When you've measured the flour, your toddler will enjoy tapping the edge of the sieve and watching the flour sprinkle into the mixture.

Greasing a tin is a good job for a toddler. Give her a piece of kitchen paper and show her how to spread the butter around the tin. You'll need to go over it again to ensure the tin is well covered. Then let her help smooth the mixture around the tin. Then – the best bit of all – give your toddler the spoon to lick. If you're worried about the raw eggs in the mixture, you could let her lick the spoon before the eggs have been added; that way she'll just get the butter and sugar.

Let your toddler carefully peep through the oven door as the cake begins to rise, and encourage her to smell it. When the cake is ready, you can serve it as it is or you could ice it (*see activity 65, Cake Art*).

How to make a sponge cake

Beat together the butter and sugar, then mix in the eggs. Sieve in the flour and baking powder and fold into the mixture. Spoon into the prepared tin or baking cases. Bake in an oven preheated to 160°C/325°F/ Gas 3 for 20 minutes. This recipe will make a small sponge cake or 12 buns (double the ingredients to make a large cake or 24 buns).

65 Cake Art

☺ | ☹

Decorating a cake can be even more fun than making it. An easy way to involve your toddler is to ice the cake yourself, then let her stick on a selection of decorations. Talk about the colours and how many sweets she's putting on the cake. At first your toddler may be happy to add just one or two sweets to the cake but, in time, she'll want to pile on the decorations.

Alternatively, you can involve your child in making the icing (*see opposite*). As with making the cake, she can help weigh the butter and pick it up and place it in the mixing bowl. She can also help to sieve the icing sugar by

What you need

- 75 g (3 oz) butter or margarine, softened
- 225 g (8 oz) icing sugar
- 2 tablespoons milk
- a few drops of food colouring

Any of the following:

- jelly sweets
- chocolate buttons
- marshmallows
- chocolate sprinkles
- hundreds and thousands

TODDLER

tapping the side of the sieve and help you mix the ingredients together. Let your child choose a colour for the icing. At this age, give your child just two options to avoid overwhelming her. It's best if you add the food colouring of her choice yourself because you only need a few drops and it's easy to accidently add too much.

Your child will probably enjoy helping to spread the icing onto the cake. Use either a spoon or palette knife. It may be a bit messy but you can cover imperfections with decorations.

As well as decorating a large cake, your toddler may also enjoy decorating her own little cake to eat straight away (children under two and a half don't have the mental capacity to understand saving things or waiting until later).

How to make icing

Sieve the icing sugar into a mixing bowl with the butter or margarine. Add the milk, then cream all the ingredients together. Add a few drops of colouring and mix together.

Benefits

Improves manual dexterity

By the age of one, your toddler will be able to pick up very small objects, like hundreds and thousands, and let go of them randomly. By fifteen months she will have the fine motor skills to let go of objects like small sweets with precision and control. Decorating a cake is a great way for your toddler to practise these skills.

Teaches about colours

Although your child is still too young to learn colours by name, choosing a colour for the icing will increase her awareness of the concept of colour. Also, selecting different-coloured sweets to decorate her cake with will increase her colour awareness.

Provides a sense of achievement

At this age, children don't yet have the skills to make very much, so being able to decorate her own cake will give your toddler a real sense of achievement and satisfaction.

66 Making Bread

Making bread is a wonderful pastime, for both your child and for you. If you use fast-acting yeast (available from supermarkets), the process is very simple. This recipe makes white bread. Give your toddler his own piece of dough to knead – he'll watch you with your dough and have great fun copying. When you shape the dough, you could try making fun shapes such as little hedgehogs. Your toddler could even add raisins for eyes. When you have finished your shapes, explain to him that the bread is going to get bigger, and return to have a look every so often.

What you need

- Baking tray, greased
- 750 g (1½ lb) strong plain flour (or bread flour)
- 25 g (1 oz) butter, softened
- 1 sachet fast-acting yeast
- 450 ml (15 fl oz) warm water

Benefits

Aids sensory development

Touching and kneading the dough and getting sticky hands will familiarize your toddler with a texture that may be unusual to him. This will help to avoid sensory problems as he gets older (*see page 111*).

Promotes healthy eating

By making your own bread you can control the salt and sugar levels – most shop-bought bread is shockingly high in salt. Plus, fresh homemade bread is so delicious it can be eaten without butter, which will help to accustom your child to eating 'dry' bread – a very healthy habit. In addition, he is likely to be less fussy about eating the crusts on homemade bread as it tends to be softer than shop-bought varieties.

Keeps costs down

Another benefit for you is that making your own bread works out cheaper than buying it ready made.

Relieves anxiety

Bread-making is the perfect activity for those days when your toddler is saying 'No' to everything and seems to be more bad-tempered and prone to tantrums than usual. Kneading bread is known to have a calming effect and he is bound to enjoy squeezing the springy dough through his hands. The rhythmic pounding and punching of dough is a great way to release your frustrations, too – and the calmer you are, the calmer your child will be. Do teach him to pound the dough because he'll find it great fun and it will help him to release his anger, too.

How to make bread

Put the butter and yeast in a large mixing bowl and sift in the flour, then stir in the water and mix into a soft dough. Turn onto a floured surface and knead well for 10 minutes. Either shape the dough to form a loaf or divide it up to make 8–10 rolls. Transfer the dough to the baking tray, cover with cling film and leave it in a warm room or airing cupboard for about 90 minutes until it has doubled in size. Remove the cling film and bake in an oven preheated to 230°C/450°F/ Gas 8 for 30–35 minutes for a loaf or 15–20 minutes for rolls. If the bread sounds hollow when you tap it, it's cooked. If you wish, you can wrap the bread in a clean tea towel while it cools, to soften the crust.

67 Where's Your Head?

Your toddler may now be quite aware of various parts of her body, like her hands and her nose. When you have a little quiet time together, you can teach her what these body parts are called. To begin with, simply touch her toes and repeat the word 'toes', then touch her head and say 'That's your head,' and so on. Just play this game for a minute or two at a time so she doesn't become tired or bored. An ideal time to try this is during bath time or a nappy change when she isn't wearing much, but it can be played at any time. You can play this game even if you are queuing at a checkout – it's a good way to distract a restless toddler.

Once your child has heard the names of a few body parts lots of times, she'll start to remember them. At this point you can progress a little and start saying things like, 'Touch your nose.' Begin with just one body part

Benefits

Boosts memory

Between the ages of one and two, your toddler's memory will improve considerably. Playing this game will stimulate her memory as she tries to memorize the words; the more the memory is stimulated, the better it becomes.

Aids language development

This is an obvious benefit: by teaching your toddler new words you are increasing her vocabulary. Understanding words is the first step to being able to say them. Because this game is interactive, you will be constantly watching

and responding to your toddler and giving her positive feedback when she can understand, and eventually say, words. A positive response is essential for babies and toddlers to develop language.

Provides a useful distraction

From about twelve months, toddlers often start to make a lot of fuss about having their nappy changed. Playing a fun word game together will help to distract her and will encourage her to lie still rather than protesting and trying to stand up.

to avoid confusion and help your toddler to point to her nose, each time saying, 'Touch your nose.' When she eventually does it herself, make sure you give her lots of praise. Then move on to another body part and gradually build up your child's listening vocabulary.

Your toddler will be ready to start learning body parts from about fourteen months, although it will be a few more months before she can grasp more than one or two. Early talkers will learn body parts more quickly, although children understand long before they can speak, so it's certainly worth spending a minute or two pointing out fingers, thumbs, toes, tummies and so on. Even late talkers will be able to play this game because it doesn't actually require them to say any words, just understand them. When she has mastered the basic body parts, you can start to teach your toddler the words for more advanced, technical ones such as elbows, cheeks and knees.

68 Bath-time Fun

You may have accumulated a collection of bath toys over the last few months. These are useful both for entertaining your toddler and teaching him about sinking and floating and the properties of water. However, if you want to try something a bit more original you could give your toddler a pair of rubber gloves to play with in the bath. Ensure they're clean and not contaminated with anything nasty like bleach. Explain what a glove is, how it fits over your hand and what rubber gloves are for. Fill a glove with water and seal the end with a freezer-bag clip, then show your toddler how the glove actually looks like a hand – he won't necessarily make the association. Have fun counting the fingers, talking about the fingers and the thumb and showing your child his own fingers and thumbs. Make the hand wave hello and goodbye. You could make a tiny hole in

What you need

Any of the following:
- Rubber gloves
- Freezer-bag clip
- Ice cubes
- Bath books

one of the fingers, then show your toddler how to squeeze water out. You could even talk about milking cows and explain where milk comes from. Have fun squirting the water over your toddler and, if he's water-confident, squeeze it over his head and face.

Another fun game is to put ice cubes in the bath and encourage your toddler to try to catch them with his hands or a cup before they melt.

From about twelve months of age your toddler will start to enjoy looking at bath books – waterproof books made for bath time. He'll like the fact that the book is wet and will also enjoy you reading a story to him while he's in the bath.

Benefits

Introduces the idea of counting
From about eighteen months your child will mimic counting if he hears it often enough. Although he won't understand the concept of numbers until he's about two and a half, being able to memorize numbers one to ten, for instance, will give him a head start.

Promotes water confidence
We've mentioned this before, but it really can't be emphasized enough how important it is to build your child's confidence in water. The key is to push your child's comfort zone just a little, but, of course, stop if he becomes upset in any way. The process should be very gradual, slowly building up water play to become increasingly boisterous.

Promotes understanding of the world
Your toddler will learn about rubber gloves, milking cows, ice and any other concepts you introduce to bath time.

Aids language development
Your toddler will learn new words effortlessly if he's fascinated by what he sees so, even if he's not saying much yet, take the time to talk to him about the rubber gloves and the ice cubes. Reading bath books to your child will also help to increase his vocabulary.

69 Walk and Talk

When you're out with your toddler, try to find ways to communicate with her as you go along, rather than just strapping her in the buggy and chatting on your mobile phone. This is particularly important now that she is learning to talk. Of course, it would be unrealistic and also quite intense to try to communicate with her for the entire outing, but if you can dedicate a few minutes to the task each time you are out together, you will both benefit a great deal. Point things out to your toddler, like cats,

What you need

- Time to look around
- Child's umbrella
- Wellington boots

dogs, diggers, fire engines – the list is endless – and stop and crouch down beside the buggy for a brief chat about what you see. Once your child starts to talk and is able to name things that she sees, you can simply ask her, 'What can you see over there?' It's also important to respond whenever your child wants to point something out to you or talk about something that has caught her attention.

Once your toddler can walk quite confidently, you can start going for short walks without the buggy. To keep things interesting, you could incorporate activities like crunching on autumn leaves, collecting conkers, acorns, sticks and stones, jumping in puddles, stamping on ice (making sure she doesn't slip),

picking some blossom and putting it in your child's button hole. The changing of the seasons will bring along a whole range of new things to see and do on your walks.

You will probably find that your toddler will be delighted if you take a small umbrella for her to hold, even if it's not raining. She will also want to walk on walls, touch fences, gates and hedges (make sure they're not prickly), and greet cats and dogs. It can take a lot longer than usual to get anywhere, but allow plenty of time and, rather than thinking of the walk as tediously slow, see it as one of your toddler's daily activities – one that is giving her fresh air and exercise – and a great way to have fun together.

Benefits

Helps strengthen bonds

When you arrive with your toddler at nursery, playgroup, or home, you will feel much closer to her and probably more relaxed if you've been having a chat or playing together along the way.

Aids language development

You'll see all kinds of things when you're out, and talking about what you see together will extend your toddler's

vocabulary and improve her language. Responding when she says something will be of huge benefit to her speech development.

Promotes understanding of the world

There's scope for teaching your toddler about all kinds of everyday occurrences, from a hole in the road being mended, to a bird catching a worm.

70 Falling Tower

What you need

- Different-sized cardboard boxes
- Sticky tape

Making a giant tower out of cardboard boxes to bash down will be great fun for your toddler. Before you begin, seal up the boxes with tape to make them nice and rigid. Help your toddler to find the biggest box to go at the bottom, then another slightly smaller box and so on. When the tower becomes too tall for him to reach the top, he can steady the boxes at the bottom while you continue to build. If the tower isn't too tall, you could put some empty toilet rolls or a soft toy at the top for your toddler to try to reach.

Benefits

Helps improve hand–eye coordination
Piling up the boxes without them toppling down requires careful handling and coordination.

Teaches mathematical skills
Learning that the biggest boxes need to go at the bottom of the tower will teach your toddler basic structural rules.

Encourages team work
Working together to make a tower will demonstrate to your toddler how people can have different roles to complete a task.

71 Stacking and Nesting

Nesting cups are a classic toy that has withstood the test of time and still proves popular with babies and toddlers. At twelve months your child will probably be able to separate out the cups, chew them and perhaps bang them together. By fifteen months his motor skills will have devleoped sufficiently to enable him to use both hands competently and so be more precise when he takes the cups apart. He is unlikely to try to put them back together until he approaches two, when he may realize that a large cup is too big to fit inside a smaller cup. In the meantime, you can demonstrate how to re-stack the cups in size order, how to make a tower of cups (that he can bash down), and perhaps count the cups.

What you need

- Nesting cups

Benefits

Improves dexterity

Taking the cups apart will improve your toddler's fine motor skills as well as his hand–eye coordination.

Teaches investigative skills

As your child takes the cups apart he will explore how their shape changes and the number of cups increases.

Teaches mathematical skills

Learning to stack the cups in size order, and eventually fitting them together in size order, will improve your child's mathematical understanding.

72 Wash-day Fun

Your child can be involved at every stage of the laundry process, and this is actually easier than trying to keep her entertained with something else while you do the washing. It may also encourage her to be independent and help with her own washing as she gets older.

When you strip the beds, your toddler can have fun crawling into an empty duvet cover. Or you can tie the corner of a sheet to a door handle, then take the other end and swish it up and down to make a breeze while your child sits underneath – a particularly welcome game on a hot day. When you've collected up the washing, get your toddler to help you transfer it from the basket to the washing machine. Then, once you've set the cycle, you could let her press the start button, although

not all parents will like this idea as it may encourage her to re-set the machine on her own. Once the washing machine is going, show your child the washing going around through the port-hole, perhaps asking her to

What you need

- Dirty laundry

identify her own clothes and watching the water and the bubbles. Explain what's happening and how the clothes are being washed.

When the cycle has finished, your toddler can help you unload the washing into the laundry basket and help to hang it up. She'll enjoy watching you skilfully shake out the washing, then hang it up neatly, and may try to imitate you.

When the washing is dry, show her how to sort it into different piles: one for each member of the family and piles of socks ready to be paired. Give your child a red sock, for instance, then ask her to find the matching one. To make it easier, just give her two to choose from; perhaps a red one and a blue one. As she approaches her second birthday she may be able to find the matching sock by herself.

You can give your toddler simple instructions throughout the laundry process. From about one year, children can follow very simple instructions, so you could ask her to pass you some clothes from the laundry basket for you to hang up. Then, as your child approaches two, she may be able to follow more complicated instructions such as, 'Put these clothes on Mommy and Daddy's bed, please.'

Benefits

Teaches cause and effect

Pressing the 'on' switch on the washing machine will demonstrate cause and effect, as will sitting under the bed sheet while you swish it to create 'wind'. The latter will also give your toddler a basic demonstration of what wind is.

Improves numerical skills

Pairing socks will give your child a rudimentary sense of numbers, as she will see two socks. Sorting the finished laundry into different piles for the family will demonstrate how to categorize and organize objects.

Teaches about colours

Although children don't tend to learn their colours before their second birthday, helping to pair up socks of different colours will raise her awareness of colours and their names.

Improves memory and concentration

Following simple requests will require your toddler to concentrate, and following more complicated two-part instructions requires both concentration and memory. If you ask her to put some washing on your bed, she will have to remember what to do once she gets into the bedroom.

73 Just Like Mommy and Daddy

From about one year, children start to copy mommy and daddy and, by the time they reach about eighteen months, they will be keen to carry out all kinds of tasks that they have seen you do, such as cooking, DIY and anything else that involves using fun-looking tools and gadgets. So, a toy kitchen or workbench is bound to be a hit. You could buy a toy kitchen, with a cooker, sink and cupboards, or you can improvise and create one using a dining chair as a hob and putting a couple of small saucepans on the seat. Give your child a wooden spoon and he'll soon start to cook. Help him by suggesting that he stirs the beans in the saucepan. Pretend

What you need

- Toy kitchen
- Toy workbench

Or any of the following:

- Wooden spoons
- Plastic bowls
- Saucepans
- Dining chair
- Toy tools
- Paintbrushes
- Bucket
- Children's table and chairs

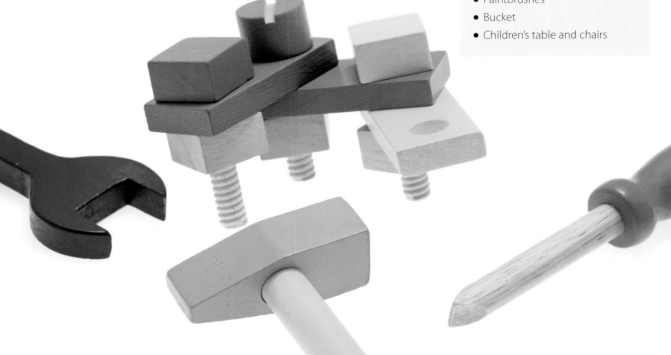

to stir them yourself, then pretend to lick the spoon and eat some. Because your child is still very young, it's useful to demonstrate clearly how he can use his imagination. You can maintain his interest by adding to his collection of kitchenware: a small whisk, a pastry brush, more spoons and so on – anything that's not sharp or dangerous.

Make-believe DIY is a little more difficult to improvise because most tools are heavy, sharp or both, so obviously unsafe for toddlers to play with. However, you could give your toddler a small, clean paintbrush and a bucket which can be his paint pot. Show him how he can pretend to paint doors, radiators and so on. You can buy toy tools and even toy workbenches – these often come complete with tools and nuts that click into holes. If your child has a few toy tools, he will love being given pretend DIY jobs to do, especially tasks that he's seen other people do. You could ask him to 'mend a radiator', 'fix a pipe' or perhaps 'saw some wood to make some shelves'.

Benefits

Improves dexterity and hand–eye coordination

Whether your toddler is stirring pots in his kitchen or sawing wood on his workbench, he'll be using his fine motor skills and developing his dexterity and hand–eye coordination.

Encourages imaginative play

Your toddler will use his imagination to visualize the food he's stirring in his saucepan, or the holes he's making with his drill. A good imagination will help with problem solving in later life, as your child will be able to think creatively and resourcefully. It will also help him to be adaptable.

74 Setting the Table

Before the age of two, your toddler won't be able to do much to help with setting the table, apart from putting the spoons out; she will certainly be too young to cope with an entire cutlery set. You can lay the knives and forks out together, then your toddler can put the spoons in place. Talk about who is going to sit where, and how each person needs a spoon so they can eat their pudding. Show her which way round to place the spoon and where to put the knife and fork. She'll probably be able to concentrate for a few minutes, perhaps longer on some days. Like helping with the laundry, learning to set the table is part of daily life and will encourage independence in the future.

What you need

- Kitchen or dining table
- Cutlery

You may also like to use:

- Roll of spare wallpaper (or cheap lining paper)
- Sticky tape
- Crayons, or paints and brushes
- Child-friendly glue
- Glitter

TODDLER

A fun way to prepare a table for a special occasion is to tape some old wallpaper (patterned side down) or lining paper to the table so that it is completely covered (it's much easier to cover a square or rectangular table than a round one), then let your toddler decorate it. Although she will be able to make a few marks on paper from about the age of one, once she reaches eighteen months she will be far more competent and free with her paintbrushes and crayons, so she'll be able to make the table extremely colourful. She'll also enjoy gluing, so let her put some glue on the paper and then give her some glitter to sprinkle on top. As well as decorating

Damage limitation

Make sure you explain to your child that you have covered the table with paper which she is allowed to draw on, but that she mustn't draw on the table if there is no paper on it.

the table for parties, this is also a fun rainy-day activity and is a lovely way to brighten up a family meal. Do allow plenty of time for the glue and paint to dry; this may take several hours as your toddler is likely to be particularly liberal with glue and paint at this age.

Benefits

Introduces the idea of planning

Preparing the table, whether you are decorating it or laying it ready for a meal, teaches your toddler to plan. She'll need to think ahead and visualize everyone sitting at the table appreciating her handy work. Anticipation requires imagination and encourages your toddler to use the thinking, cognitive part of her brain.

Helps mathematical development

Laying the table will teach your child about logic by demonstrating that everyone needs a bowl and a spoon to eat

their pudding – 'a spoon for Mommy, a spoon for Daddy and a spoon for Charlie' and so on. This will help her to understand the meaning of numbers, which is far more complex than simply learning to count by mimicking.

Improves dexterity

Any kind of drawing or painting helps children to develop their hand–eye coordination, preparing them to learn to write. Show your child how to hold the crayon or paintbrush like a pen. If she's not yet comfortable doing this, leave it for a while and try showing her again in a month or so.

75 Playdough

Playdough is available in toy shops and supermarkets; however, not only is it great fun to make your own, it also saves money, you will have lots of it and, if you keep it in a sealed container in the fridge, it will last for months. The simple method shown below makes good bouncy playdough (thanks to the cream of tartar and oil) and the lavender, if you choose to use it, will give off a wonderful aroma as your child plays with the dough. Make sure it is cool before you let your toddler touch it, then have fun squeezing and playing with the dough. This may be all she wants to do at first but, once she gets used to it, show her how to roll it into balls and worms, which she can try to coil. Then you can progress to using a rolling pin and pastry cutters; you could even help her to squeeze some dough through a garlic press.

You can make all kinds of shapes. Try forming the dough into a hedgehog shape, for example, then sticking in lots of cut-up straws to make prickles and stick on plastic eyes or simply mark on eyes with a pencil.

Another fun activity is to go on a nature walk and collect feathers, flowers, leaves and stones, and anything else you can find. Then stick them into a lump of playdough.

You could make playdough eggs and put them into egg cups, then pretend to eat them. It may take a few attempts to get the size right, but talk it through with your child – 'this egg is too big for the egg cup', 'this egg is too small', and so on.

How to make your own playdough

Mix together a mug of plain flour, half a mug of salt and 2 teaspoons of cream of tartar. Then add 2 mugs of water and 2 teaspoons of cooking oil. If you wish, you can add a few drops each of food colouring and lavender aromatherapy oil. When all the ingredients are well combined, put the dough in the microwave and heat on full power for one minute. Stir, then heat for another minute. The dough should become stretchy and too thick to stir. You may need to heat it for another 30 seconds. Knead the mixture thoroughly until the dough is very smooth.

No microwave?

If you don't have a microwave, heat the dough in a saucepan on a gentle heat, stirring continually until the dough becomes stretchy and too thick to stir.

What you need

- Playdough

Any of the following:

- Rolling pin
- Pastry cutters
- Garlic press
- Straws
- Plastic eyes
- Feathers
- Leaves
- Flowers
- Stones

Benefits

Has a calming effect

The scent of lavender is known to have a soothing effect on the brain, so your toddler may become calmer as she inhales the scent. The sensory act of kneading the dough and squeezing it through her fingers may also help your child to relax.

Teaches about scale

Making an egg the right size to fit an egg cup will teach your toddler about scale and size.

Improves dexterity

Rolling, cutting and sticking things like straws and feathers into the playdough will help to develop your toddler's fine motor skills.

76 Merry Dance

Once your child has been walking for a few months and is reasonably steady on her feet, she is ready to dance, so switch on the radio or put on a CD and dance with your toddler. Hold her hands while she dances and pick her up and spin her around. Then step back so that you can dance separately —she may copy your moves! At this age your child will dance enthusiastically and won't be at all self-conscious; do encourage her so that dancing becomes part of family life as she grows up.

Benefits

Taps into her natural rhythm

All children have natural rhythm at this age and by dancing together you will help her to tap into this skill. Learning to dance at this age is much easier than at three or four when your child will become socially aware and may be a bit self-conscious.

Boosts stamina

Dancing is a fun way for small children to expend excess energy, which makes it the perfect rainy-day exercise.

What you need

- Music

77 Catch Me if you Can!

By eighteen months, some toddlers are able to run quite quickly and can also change direction, so this is the ideal time to try playing a game of chase. Playing outside is ideal; alternatively, you could run around a table after your toddler, changing directions every now and again to take her by surprise.

What you need

- Outside space
- If indoors, a table

Benefits

Boosts stamina
This is a good way for your toddler to expend some excess energy, and as she runs she will boost her fitness and stamina levels.

Improves reaction times
Your toddler will have to dodge out of the way to avoid getting caught and this will help to speed up her reaction times.

Teaches about judgement and planning
As your toddler learns to run behind a table to avoid getting caught, she'll develop her judgement and planning skills. She will work out that when you change direction she needs to as well, so will run around the table in the opposite direction.

78 Tidy Toddlers

Small children love helping around the house and there's plenty that they can do. To begin with, get your toddler to put pairs of shoes together, particularly her own. If you have a lot of shoes lying around, you can make this into a great game of match the shoe. It's particularly useful to teach your toddler to put her shoes in the same place whenever she takes them off – this will help to avoid a frantic shoe hunt when you're going out and are running late.

Putting toys away can also be made into a fun game. By the age of one, children are able to use their hands independently and so have the ability to put things into boxes – even quite small objects such as bricks. You can say to your toddler, 'Let's put the toys away together', then start crashing the bricks into a box. She'll love joining in, especially if you make a big deal about the crashing noise that the bricks make.

Your toddler is still too young to be expected, or in any way pressured, to tidy up her toys, but you

What you need

Any of the following:

- Pairs of shoes
- Storage boxes
- Dustpan and brush or a toy broom
- Cloth or kitchen paper

can entice her into helping you by making the task fun. A tidying-up song often works very well. You could try making one up and singing it whenever it's time to start clearing things away; your toddler will immediately know that it's time to end the game and tidy up. By about twenty months, children are able to do very simple puzzles, so why not make a puzzle out of clearing things away? If you've been playing with animals and vehicles, explain that animals go in one box and vehicles go in the other, then solve the puzzle together. Through repeated exposure to these toys, your toddler will know that animals have faces and that they eat and sleep, and vehicles have wheels, are made of metal and make a 'brrrm' noise.

Also from the age of about twenty months, your child will love copying you when she sees you carrying out a task such as sweeping. Of course, she won't yet have the skills to sweep the floor herself, but you could give her a dustpan and brush to play with, perhaps even allowing her to hold the dustpan while you sweep the bits into it. You could also give your toddler her own toy broom.

Washing windows can also be made into a great game. While you toil away, you could give your toddler a cloth or a piece of kitchen paper so that she can polish too.

Benefits

Aids mathematical development
Pairing shoes together involves identifying any that are the same and understanding that you only need to find two of each. This is a good early step in teaching your child the concept of numbers.

Teaches sorting skills
Putting toys away in boxes involves picking up and putting down small objects with precision. To sort cars and bricks into two different boxes, your toddler will need organizing and categorizing skills so that she can recognize and classify each object.

Boosts understanding of the world
Sweeping floors and washing windows will teach your toddler about housework – a part of life that isn't going to go away when she's older, whether or not she chooses to do any!

79 Furry Friends

In activity 46, Animal Fun, we talked about how to familiarize your child with dogs and cats so that he isn't afraid of them. As he approaches two, he will become less impulsive and able to stay still for longer periods, so you can start to introduce him to various small animals. He can look at hamsters, rabbits or guinea pigs in their cage and you can explain how they need food and water, just like him. Let your toddler help to fill the water bottles and food dishes. He'll love the idea of being in charge of a small animal.

When it comes to petting small animals, your toddler will still need a lot of supervision to avoid the animal being roughly handled or escaping. You'll also want to ensure that your toddler

What you need

Any of the following:

- Friends with pets or your own small pet
- Food scraps
- Bird feed
- Stale bread

doesn't get bitten or nipped, which could be upsetting for him. Begin by holding the animal and letting your toddler stroke it using just one finger. If you've got a particularly docile pet, you may be able to let your toddler hold it, as long as your hands are hovering very close by.

If you don't have a small pet or any friends who own pets, you could pack up some stale brown bread to feed the ducks at your local park (check that this is permitted). Or, if you have a garden, you could feed

the birds with food scraps or bird feed. If you do this in the winter, take care to continue throughout the cold months as the birds may have come to depend on you as a food source so could go hungry if you stop feeding them.

Benefits

Improves dexterity

To stroke a small animal gently requires dexterity and good fine motor skills. Handling a wriggling pet (albeit with help) requires skill and coordination. Touching and handling small pets will also help your child to become familiar with animals like rabbits, hamsters and mice and to feel comfortable around them rather than nervous or afraid.

Teaches about responsibility

Nurturing small animals will help to give your toddler an introduction to responsibility. This will obviously be limited at this age, although feeding pets and giving them drinks will certainly help to develop the concept of looking after living things. It will also give him a sense that he has some control in the world and an important role. He will learn that he can't always control pets in the way that he does his toys – small pets escape from cages, pigeons fly away, ducks don't always swim over to be fed. This can be difficult for a young child to cope with, but it's an important part of their learning.

Increases understanding of nature

As your toddler learns that his pet needs food and water, he'll begin to understand about the survival needs of living creatures. Likewise, when he feeds birds or ducks, he'll understand the concept of being alive and how animals are different to toys.

80 Creative Scribbles

From around eighteen months your toddler will have the skills needed to scribble enthusiastically with chunky crayons. Once she can use these easily, try progressing to pencils and pens. Draw some pictures for your toddler; she'll love recognizing dogs, trees, houses, faces and so on, and you can let her add the eyes or perhaps a tail, or scribble on some hair. At this age, children have the ability to draw dots, so you could draw a picture of someone with an umbrella and your toddler could add the rain.

Benefits

Boosts hand–eye coordination

As your child practises scribbling and drawing, she will gain better control of her drawing hand, especially as her hand–eye coordination improves.

Promotes creativity

If your child helps you to draw recognizable pictures, she'll see the potential of what can be done with a pencil and paper. Scribbling independently allows her to take her first rudimentary creative steps.

What you need

- Chunky crayons
- Paper (scrap is fine)
- Children's table and chair or highchair

Which hand?

Children should be ambidextrous until they are at least eighteen months old. They start to favour one hand over the other any time between eighteen months and five years.

81 Tinfoil People

What you need

- Tinfoil

Benefits

Boosts understanding of the world
As your toddler watches a flat piece of foil turn into a person, she'll see how shape and form can change.

Aids language development
Guessing what the foil is going to turn into will encourage your toddler to talk, even if she's usually hesitant about speaking.

This is an instant way to amuse a toddler. A sheet of tinfoil can be bent and moulded into various shapes for your toddler to guess what you're making. If you make a tinfoil man, she can have fun bending the legs and arms and even making the man kick a tinfoil football or walk a tinfoil dog. She can also have a go at moulding her own characters and shapes, although at this age she will need some help.

You can also use tinfoil shapes to supplement your toddler's toys. A toy farm can have tinfoil milk churns, and a garage can have tinfoil tools to mend the cars.

What you need

A selection from the following:

- Banana, peeled
- Orange, sliced in half
- Lemon, sliced in half
- Ground cinnamon
- Cut flowers
- Sprig of rosemary
- Sprig of lavender
- Bay leaf
- Toothpaste
- Soap
- Shampoo
- Perfume

82 What's that Smell?

Sense of smell is already developed at birth, but at around eighteen months children learn to actually sniff. You can encourage your toddler to smell all kinds of things. Take a cut orange, for instance, when you're in the kitchen, smell it yourself first and describe the smell – sweet, fresh, juicy and so on. Then, when you have your child's attention, invite her to smell it too. If you're out with the buggy and happen to walk past a lavender or rosemary bush, break off a sprig, show your toddler how you can crush it between your fingers to release the smell, then give it to her to hold and sniff. Try to introduce your toddler to as many different smells as possible – a new bar of soap, your perfume, toothpaste, a new book. The list is endless.

Once your toddler is used to the idea that different objects have different smells, you can play 'What's that smell?' So, if you walk past that lavender or rosemary bush, break off a sprig and, without letting her see it,

ask, 'What's that smell?' You'll be amazed at how quickly she learns to recognize smells.

Even if you don't play this game, smell will undoubtedly play an important part in your child's life. For example, lots of children have a favourite toy that they take to bed and, if this applies to your toddler, you may well have found that if you wash it she gets annoyed because it smells different. This is because children can find comfort in smells.

Benefits

Develops the olfactory sense

Once you start to familiarize your toddler with different smells, she will soon become aware that everything has a different smell. As she practises, she will begin to recognize and learn a wide range of smells, her nose will become more attuned to different scents and she will become more sensitive to them.

Raises understanding of the world

As your toddler delves further into the world of smell, her knowledge will expand: for example, she might learn that crushing herbs brings out the smell, that fruits release their scent when you cut them up, and that some flowers have a strong fragrance but others don't smell at all. Of course, this

all seems obvious to adults but to children it's all new information to be learnt.

Provides comfort

You can use smells to help calm your toddler down. If she's upset, encourage her to smell her comfort toy by putting it close to her face.

Aids language development

The 'What's that smell?' game is a fun way to learn new words. Your child may learn quite complicated, unusual words that she wouldn't otherwise have come across at this age.

83 Lipstick Art

Painting your child's lips with lipstick and getting her to kiss a piece of brightly coloured card is a fun way to make some great pictures. This activity will appeal to your toddler most once she reaches about eighteen months and is able to pucker up her lips. By this age she shouldn't be tempted to bite the lipstick, although the idea of putting on Mommy's lipstick may be quite attractive!

Begin by practising on scrap paper. Paint your own lips, kiss the paper to leave a mark, then paint your toddler's lips and get her to have a go at kissing the paper. She'll be thrilled that it leaves a mark. Then you can show her how you can make different lip prints by forming your mouth into different shapes: an 'oooh' sound, an 'eee' sound, an open-mouth shape and a closed-mouth 'mmm' shape.

Once your toddler has got the hang of making lipstick prints, you can get her to kiss brightly coloured card. Good combinations are yellow card with pink and orange lipstick, and orange card with pink lipstick.

What you need
- Orange, pink and red lipsticks
- Yellow and orange card
- Yellow and orange envelopes
- Picture frames

You can make some great pictures that can be turned into greetings cards for your family or framed and put on the wall. The cards will look particularly effective if you put them in matching orange or yellow envelopes, especially if you show your toddler how to seal them with a loving kiss!

A variation on this game is to kiss a steamed-up mirror or window and encourage your child to make different-shaped patterns with her lips. You could also show her how to draw finger pictures on the glass. Although your toddler is too young to draw specific shapes and pictures, she will have fun scribbling and making marks.

Benefits

Promotes creativity

Your toddler will be particularly proud of her lipstick picture because it will be all her own work. Before the age of two she won't be capable of making specific, controlled marks with a pencil or paintbrush, but printing with her lips is something she will be able to control. This will give her a sense of achievement, which will help her creative development.

Assists speech development

Lip printing is a technique used by speech therapists to teach children how to make their lips into different shapes for speech and sound production. For example, we push our lips forward to make sounds such as 'oo', 'sh' and 'w'.

Encouraging your toddler to kiss will teach her to move her lips forward. Getting her to make open-mouth shapes will help her with sounds such as 'ee', and a closed-mouth shape helps with the sound 'mm'. Making different lipstick shapes on the card gets your toddler to move her lips rapidly and gain control over them, which is important for speech development.

Controls dribbling

Good lip control can sometimes help to control dribbling. Some toddlers continue to dribble until they're about three or four, when they start to become socially aware. Don't worry if your child still dribbles; it simply means she has a lot of saliva.

84 Let's Pretend Library

Visiting a library with your toddler is a wonderful activity. He'll enjoy the outing and, more importantly, he'll learn to love books as he'll be excited by the choice and will see other children looking at books. He'll also be thrilled that he is allowed to take books home. If he's particularly interested in something – animals, perhaps – find him some animal books and let him choose which ones to take home.

When you get home, set up a pretend library together. Insert labels into the front of some of your toddler's books for stamping – self-adhesive notes work well for this. If your child has a printing set, you could stamp the labels, taking care not to get any ink on

What you need

- Books
- Self-adhesive notes
- Printing set or a potato and some paint

the books themselves (it doesn't matter if you don't stamp the date; any stamp will do). Otherwise you could use half a potato and a little paint in a dish, or improvise with a tube of hand cream which will work perfectly well as a pretend stamp, especially if you embellish the process with a stamping noise (just click your tongue). Explain to your toddler how he can choose a book, have it stamped and take it home to read. You'll probably find that he prefers being the librarian and stamping the books that you borrow, but you can encourage him to take turns.

Make the most of your library

Look out for community activities such as story-telling or nursery-rhyme sessions at your local library.

Benefits

Encourages self-control

Stamping library books will fire up your child's imagination and encourage him to enjoy make-believe play. When toddlers play this kind of game, they usually behave beyond their age and are more likely to follow adult rules and social norms and expectations. This helps them to self-regulate their behaviour. Put simply, if your child is pretending to be a librarian stamping books in a quiet library, he's unlikely to have a tantrum and hurl the books on the floor, because he knows that's not what librarians do.

Promotes the idea of taking turns

Encouraging your toddler to take turns with the library stamp will help him to play well with other children. Although he won't have the developmental maturity to share unsupervised until he is about two and a half, it's important to introduce the concept in the meantime and to give him praise if he does manage to share.

Boosts understanding of the world

Visiting a library and playing libraries at home will teach your child how libraries work and he'll gradually come to understand the concept of borrowing and how this is different to buying something. Encouraging your toddler to follow up his interests by looking at books on the subject will help to extend his knowledge. He will also become familiar with non-fiction books and understand that they can be a source of learning.

85 Play Café

What you need

- Toy tea set
- Plastic cups
- Plastic measuring jug
- Teaspoons
- Soft toys
- Sheets of A4 paper
- Sticky tape
- Pink and yellow tissue paper

If you go to a café with your toddler, you can re-enact the experience when you get home. To make it more authentic, you could even pick up a few paper napkins and a couple of coffee stirrers. Make your home café similar to the one you visit with your toddler: if there's table service, do this at home; if you select at a counter, set up a counter at home (a couple of dining chairs pushed together will suffice). Then play out the order of events. So, with a table-service café, you sit at a table, you look at a menu, you give your order, you drink your drink and you pay your money. Or, with counter service, you queue at the counter, you make your

order, you pay your money, you collect your drink, you find a table and you drink your drink. Take turns serving and being served. Your toddler might like to use soft toys as extra customers.

As well as selling drinks, you could introduce food to your café. Ice cream is popular with most children and it's possible to make a pretend ice cream cone in seconds: roll a piece of A4 paper into a cone and fasten it with sticky tape, then take a sheet of pink tissue paper, roll it into a large, loose ball and stuff it into the cone – hey presto, you have a strawberry ice cream! Use yellow tissue paper for vanilla flavour.

For added fun (and perhaps mess), you could put some water in a measuring jug or teapot so that your toddler can actually pour the drinks. This obviously works best outdoors.

Benefits

Boosts understanding of the world
Playing cafés will teach your toddler about seemingly mundane events which, to her, are new and exciting, such as queuing, making an order, paying and stirring milk or sugar into coffee. These simple everyday events are part of your child's learning.

Teaches about sequencing
There's a certain order of doing things in cafés, and playing out this order will teach your toddler about the sequencing of events.

Develops imagination
Pretending to eat and drink requires imagination. Your toddler has to imagine that her paper ice cream is real and that she is really eating it, or that her empty cup really contains a drink that she is drinking. This requires thought and imagination and exercises the brain.

Teaches how to pour
If you use water, your toddler will learn how to pour, which requires coordination and judgement. This takes practice. She'll also learn about the scientific principle that water always finds its own level.

Boosts memory
When you place your order with your toddler, she'll have to remember what you said, 'prepare' your food and drinks and bring them to you. At this age she will probably only be able to remember one thing at a time.

86 Let's Play Shops

By now your toddler is probably very familiar with going shopping and will have a reasonable understanding of how shops work, so at this stage it can be fun to make pretend shops at home. A fun shop to re-create is the grocer's. Begin by raiding your kitchen. Gather together a collection of tins and packets from your food cupboards, and perhaps some fruit and vegetables and even an empty egg box or orange juice carton. You could also use any toy food you may have, but this isn't essential. Then let your toddler decide what she wants to 'buy for her lunch' or 'have for her dinner'. She can pretend to pay for the food and put it in her shopping bag to take home. You could use toy money which your toddler could keep in an old purse, but if you haven't got any then you could make your own (*see below right*).

As your toddler approaches her second birthday, she may like to have a go at making a shopping list. Of course, she won't be able to write, but she may have fun making a few scribbles in a notepad. You can show her how to hold the pen correctly, although don't worry at this stage if she can't manage this.

Another shop to try making at home is a shoe shop. This works well once your toddler is walking and has visited a real shoe shop to have her feet measured and to buy shoes. Gather up a collection of shoes and slippers (avoid heels because your toddler could trip), then arrange the shoes into pairs. You can measure your toddler's feet with a tape measure, then let her try on the shoes. Mom and dad's will be too big, but when she finds a pair she likes you can put them in a shoe box to 'take home'. Then let your toddler have a turn at being the shop keeper, measuring your feet and so on. You'll 'discover' that when you try to put your toddler's shoes on they are too small. Spend a little time talking about the size of shoes and feet – too big, too small and so on.

What you need

- Toy money
- An old purse
- Shopping bag
- Notepad

For a food shop:

- Tins and packets of food
- Fruit and vegetables
- Toy food

For a shoe shop:

- Shoes
- Tape measure
- Shoe boxes

How to make toy money

Cut out some cardboard circles from a cereal box or other cardboard packaging and cover with tinfoil. To make bank notes, just use a few pages from a notepad – you don't need anything elaborate.

Benefits

Improves coordination

From around twelve months, toddlers learn to hold three objects at once, so if your child is holding two grocery items, one in each hand, and you pass her a third, she will no longer drop one of the items but, instead, put one of them in the crook of the opposite arm, then take the new object with her free hand. Making a point of passing your toddler a third item will encourage and develop this skill.

Develops imagination

A pretend shop will help your toddler to develop her imagination. Imaginative play is a step towards fantasy play, which involves children playing together and taking on different roles, something your toddler will enjoy from about the age of three.

Boosts understanding of the world

Your toddler will begin to learn about the concept of money and buying things from shops.

Introduces writing

Practising 'writing' on a notepad will teach your toddler how to hold a pen, and also help her to understand the concept of writing.

87 Let's Pretend Office

Toddlers are fascinated by paperwork and computers; to them it all looks so wonderfully grown-up. However, papers and computers are usually out of bounds, which is why it can be fun to set up an office for your toddler, or perhaps a post office, as both of these involve 'off-limits' paper-work. Choose whatever your child is familiar with, so if you or your partner work from home, a pretend office is ideal. You could even set it up in your own home office, letting your toddler play with an old keyboard, mouse, mouse mat, phone, notebook, and pen while you work. She'll have fun mimicking you, but

What you need

Any of the following:

- Old keyboard
- Old mouse and mouse mat
- Old phone or toy phone
- Notepad
- Pencil
- Large cardboard box
- Collection of junk mail
- Paper
- Envelopes
- Sticky labels
- Cloth or paper bag (the larger the better)

be prepared for lots of interruptions; there's no point embarking on a complicated piece of work while your toddler is in the room. Explain to her what you are doing, even if it's just internet shopping or sending an email to daddy – you could let her click on the mouse to send the email.

Posting letters is something that we suggested your baby gets involved with in activity 36, Mommy's Helper. Now that she's old enough to enjoy imaginary games, you could take things a step further and make a postbox out of a large cardboard box and collect up junk mail for her to post, then collect up and open. She could also empty the letters from the postbox into her postman's sack (a cloth or paper bag) and deliver them to you, your partner or even a few cuddly toys. You could also give your toddler some envelopes and stamps made from sticky labels – cut these into squares and draw on a quick stamp design. Encourage her to write some letters, even if the message consists of only a scribble.

Benefits

Encourages mimicking

As your toddler watches you working in your office or opening or posting letters, she'll absorb what she sees and will imitate certain actions. Giving her props, such as a computer mouse or phone, will encourage this. Mimicking is a fundamental part of learning.

Introduces the concept of writing

Of course, your child is too young to write, but becoming familiar with pens and paper is the first step to learning this skill. Understanding that it's possible to communicate by writing, and learning what writing actually is, will also help.

Helps prepare for school

Make-believe play provides a very good grounding for formal education, which will be a big bonus once she starts school. This type of play teaches children self-control and self-regulation: as your toddler mimics you using a computer keyboard or opening your post, she will behave in a 'grown-up' way, being more self-regulated and controlled than she would normally. This will mean that, when she eventually starts school, she'll be familiar with controlling her behaviour and should be unlikely to jump about and fidget during quiet time.

88 Little Cook

From around eighteen months, your toddler can help you to prepare meals in the kitchen. There are plenty of safe jobs for her to join in with. She doesn't have to help you to make an entire meal – indeed, this would make things quite difficult for you – but helping you for a few minutes here and there with the easier jobs will provide her with lots of entertainment and interest.

Here are some ideas for how she can help. Firstly, washing vegetables, salad or fruit is a good task for toddlers to join in with. If you stand her on a step-stool so that she can reach the sink, she can have fun washing the mud off potatoes and scrubbing them or rinsing lettuce leaves in a colander. Once her nicely cleaned potatoes are cooked, she might like to help with some mashing; if you're adding any butter or herbs she could assist with this too. Likewise, she can also help to mash carrots with a little butter and perhaps a little nutmeg or ground coriander. Of course, you will need to give the vegetables a bit more of a mash afterwards.

Making a salad is a nice job for a toddler to help with. She can stir the dressing and even taste a little to help decide if it needs more oil or vinegar. In fact, she can taste the salad at any time as she mixes it, perhaps trying a little lettuce, a butter bean, some pepper and so on. If there's a vegetable that your toddler isn't particularly keen on, get her to add it to a salad – she doesn't have to eat it, just become familiar with it. You never know, she may eventually try it of her own accord.

Other fun activities that your toddler will enjoy include: peeling shells off hard-boiled eggs; helping to layer a lasagne by spooning in the mince and the cheese sauce and spreading out the pasta sheets. There are a huge number of jobs that your toddler can help you with in the kitchen. She won't be competent and will need constant supervision, but she'll like being involved.

What you need

- Plenty of time
- A meal to prepare

Getting a taste for it

Take any opportunity to encourage your toddler to taste your cooking as you prepare meals. She only has to try a tiny amount and this is a fun way to get her used to the flavours of family meals.

Benefits

Helps combat fussy eating

Being involved with food preparation can encourage picky toddlers to be a bit more adventurous when it comes to what they will eat. The more familiar your toddler becomes with a particular ingredient, the more likely she is to agree to try it, and helping in the kitchen is a particularly good way to familiarize her with a new food.

Aids dexterity

Stirring, adding spices and herbs, pouring, mashing and so on all require reasonably skilled hands. You'll pay far closer attention to your toddler's manual skills than if she was simply playing with toys, because you want the job done properly and without spills and breakages. This one-to-one intensive course will be particularly good for your toddler's fine motor development.

89 Story Time

We mentioned reading stories in Part Two (activity 29, Book Worm). Once your toddler starts talking, he will become far more involved in story time and will gradually interact more and more. From about twenty months, children are able to 'label' pictures, so if you're reading a picture book together and you say 'Where's the ball?', he'll look at the pictures and, if he knows the word, will touch the picture of the ball. Give your child lots of praise when he gets it right. When he doesn't know the word, show him the correct picture and say the new word several times. If you keep returning to this new word, your child will soon point out the correct picture. You can play this game with any book. Just ask your child, 'Where's the wolf?' 'Where's the dog?' and so on. He'll love pointing things out and getting your approval when he's right. It's best to keep these labelling sessions short – about ten minutes is plenty – because your child will find them quite tiring. And don't worry if your child wants to return to the same book time and again for a labelling

What you need

- Story books
- Picture books with one-word labels

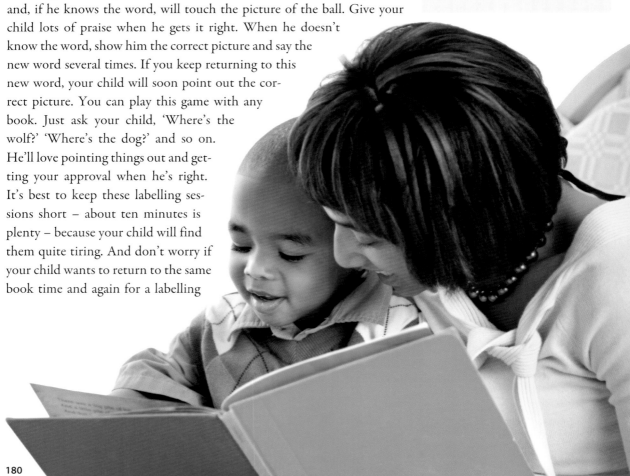

session. The comfort he'll get from the repetition is more important than pushing him to extend his vocabulary.

Once your child's speech has developed enough for him to be able to say about fifty words, you can suggest that you switch roles – he names and you point at the correct picture.

Another way to get your child to interact with books before he's talking is to encourage him to make the sounds in the story. So, if someone knocks on the door, you can show him how to knock on the back of the book. Or, if it's raining in the story, you and your child could patter your fingers on the page to make the sound of rain. This will get a dialogue going about the story even before your child can speak.

If your child has a book that he particularly likes and is familiar with, you could try reciting the story and leaving a 'blank' to see if he can say the missing word. For example, 'Hello Mr Dog, how are you .....?' in this case 'today'. This works particularly well with rhyming, rhythmic books. If you've memorized the book yourself, you can recite to your child any time of the day: for example, in the car or when you're changing his nappy.

Benefits

Aids language development
Labelling pictures will really accelerate language learning and it's a fun way for children to extend their vocabulary. This is the first stage of communicating together about books and will eventually encourage your child to talk about his books.

Boosts concentration and memory
If you teach your child new words, he'll have to concentrate in order to learn and remember them, and if he fills in the missing words as you recite the story, he'll be using his memory. This will also encourage him to say the words himself.

Has a soothing effect
If your child is upset or on the verge of a tantrum, suddenly reciting a familiar story can be a wonderful distraction technique. He'll be surprised to hear it out of context and this will probably be enough to divert him from whatever he was getting upset about.

90 Sing Along

We mentioned singing in Part Two (activity 27, Enjoy a Song). From around eighteen months, toddlers start to sing some of the words. Begin by singing a song repeatedly – you can use a nursery rhyme book or CD to jog your memory if necessary. Then, when your child is familiar with that song, start leaving out a word for her to fill in. For example, 'Heads, shoulders, knees and ....' Hopefully your child will excitedly call out 'toes!' Eventually she may attempt to sing the whole song. Try using props and actions to jog her memory.

Benefits

Boosts memory

Learning songs will help to develop your child's memory, and the more she uses her memory, the better it will become.

Improves musical ability

As your toddler learns to sing she will use her voice to copy a melody. This will require her to listen carefully to the different notes.

What you need

● A nursery rhyme book or CD

91 Drinking Straws

From around eighteen months of age your toddler will be capable of drinking through a straw, so you could try putting her milk or water in a cup or beaker without a lid and giving her a straw. If the straw is long, you may want to cut it so it's more manageable for her. As well as encouraging your child to drink through the straw, you can also show her how to blow bubbles into her drink.

If she struggles to use the straw properly, check that the end hasn't been chewed – this would indicate that she's holding it with her teeth rather than her lips.

What you need

- Drinking straws
- A healthy drink

Benefits

Aids speech development

Blowing and sucking help to strengthen the soft palate (situated behind the hard palate). The soft palate moves during speech to prevent air passing up the nasal passages and causing a nasal tone. Blowing candles, bubbles and party blowers are beneficial too.

92 Dressing Up

As your toddler approaches her second birthday she'll become increasingly interested in dressing up, and start wanting to put on her own costumes. You can buy all kinds of children's dressing-up outfits; it's worthwhile trying second-hand shops, jumble sales or online auctions if you want to keep the cost down. However, you don't need to buy an entire costume; a single item such as a policeman's helmet or an animal mask will be sufficient. These are nice and easy for your toddler to put on and take off, so at this age it's actually better to gather together a collection of accessories rather than complete outfits.

You will find that your toddler can have great fun dressing up without the need for you to buy anything at all. You've probably got lots of things around your home that she could dress up in; slippers, shoes, a hat, a cycling helmet, swimming goggles, a shower cap or a pretty night dress will intrigue your toddler, especially if she sees you putting them on. Don't worry if your little boy is drawn to your gold shoes and lacy bra – at this age, lots of little boys love pretty, sparkly things and it is no indication of your son's future sexuality. Likewise, don't be alarmed if your daughter wants to dress up as a builder.

It's also very easy to make costumes. You can create a set of fairy wings by cutting the shape out of the side of a cardboard box, then attaching them with two elastic loops which your child's arms go through, like a rucksack. Decorate the wings with paint, glitter and feathers. You can make a tail by cutting one leg off a pair of tights and stuffing it with balls of newspaper or, alternatively, you could take a piece of fur trim and simply tuck one end down the top of your toddler's trousers. Do think creatively when you're sorting out clothes to go to charity. The skirt of an old party dress could be cut into a wonderful fairy or batman cloak; a cloak can also be made from a bath towel or baby blanket.

What you need

A selection from the following:

- Children's sunglasses; toy builder's helmet; toy builder's jacket
- Fairy wings; fairy skirt
- Animal costume such as a rabbit, cat, dog or bear
- Wig
- Hat
- Slippers
- Shoes
- Costume jewellery
- Swimming goggles
- Swimming hat
- Cycling helmet
- Cardboard box
- Elastic
- Fur trimmings
- Baby blanket
- Bath towel

Benefits

Helps teach how to get dressed

Most children find it easier to get undressed than dressed, but as your toddler approaches two she will start to master the art of putting some garments on. Having a selection of dressing-up clothes will encourage your toddler to practise these skills, and help her learn to get dressed in her normal clothes.

Boosts imagination

Dressing up sparks the imagination and will allow your child to imitate adults. Perhaps she'll want to dress up as a builder or a workman and pretend to do their job. As we've said, using the imagination makes the brain think more and boosts its development. As your child rummages around, trying to find what she needs to look the part, she may find her toy hammer but if she can't find any toy nails she may improvise with crayons. Improvisation is a key part of dressing-up activities and helps children to think creatively. This will help with problem solving in the future.

93 A Day with Teddy

This is a lovely game to play with your toddler as she approaches two years and her speech is quite developed. The game simply involves your toddler's favourite teddy, cuddly toy or doll shadowing her for the day. Encourage her to be in charge of teddy, telling the toy what to do and, perhaps, reassuring him from time to time.

Your toddler can begin first thing in the morning by putting a nappy on teddy and perhaps some clothes (old baby clothes or doll's clothes will do, or even just a hat). Then teddy can join her for breakfast: he can have his own bowl and spoon, and perhaps even a little bit of dry cereal; your toddler can feed teddy if she wants. She could perhaps take him out in the buggy: give her an extra blanket to keep him warm. If you attend a toddler group, teddy could have a little nap while your child plays with the other children. Teddy could join your toddler for lunch: put a few

What you need

- A favourite cuddly toy or doll
- Baby clothes
- Nappy

Benefits

Helps speech development

Explaining to teddy what's going on during the day gives your toddler lots of talking practice. Even if she only says a few words, she'll listen to you intently as you talk to teddy.

Teaches patience

Toddlers have almost no patience before the age of two because they don't have the cognitive skills to reason and wait for what they want. However, using teddy can sometimes help a little because teaching is a proven method of

learning, so if your toddler is teaching teddy to be patient she may learn a little patience herself.

Provides reassurance

Children can find a lot of comfort and reassurance from their teddy (or other favourite soft toy). Being in charge of the teddy means that your child's role is to be brave and look after the bear if he becomes frightened. This in itself can help your child to feel more confident about worrying situations because she'll see herself as being brave.

vegetables into teddy's bowl and teddy could either eat them all up like a good little bear, or perhaps he doesn't like vegetables and your toddler has to demonstrate how delicious they are (reverse psychology can sometimes work!). At nap time, teddy can sleep in your toddler's cot with her. Tell her that she must explain to teddy that it's time to sleep and that he must be very quiet.

And so the day continues. Do encourage your toddler to explain to teddy about any 'sticking points' of your daily routine. For example, she may have to say to teddy just before tea time, 'I know you're hungry but tea will be just a few more minutes.' Your child's language won't be up to articulating this quite so clearly, but she'll get the gist. You, too, can tell teddy he must wait for his tea, then ask your child to look after teddy because he's feeling hungry and finding it difficult to wait for his tea.

94 Hide-and-Seek

This is a time-tested children's game that your toddler will no doubt have lots of fun playing. The basic principle of the game is that one person, the seeker, closes their eyes and counts, while the others run off and hide. Then the seeker opens their eyes, shouts 'coming, ready or not', then searches for the others.

A child under the age of two will struggle with the rules and get in a muddle at first because there are several stages to the game: closing her eyes, counting and then searching. And, when it's her turn to hide, she's likely to count or shout 'ready or not' from her hiding place. So, you can

What you need

- A few very obvious adult-sized hiding places
- Two adults

begin with a very simple version, asking your toddler, 'Where's Daddy?', and she can dig dad out from under the duvet. Then you can progress to 'Where's Daddy?' when dad could be in one of a number of places: under the table, behind the sofa or behind a door, perhaps. Make it very easy to find dad or your toddler will lose heart. Once your child has grasped the general idea, you can have a go at counting together. As she approaches her second birthday she even may start to join in the counting if she hears it often enough.

The next step is to let your toddler have a go at hiding. She's bound to select the hiding places that dad chose, but this doesn't matter. Before the age of two, your toddler probably won't have the self-control or the understanding to wait while you count and then hunt for her, or while you hide, which is why you may well need a second adult or older child to wait with her.

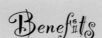

Benefits

Teaches about counting

Although your toddler may be able to mimic counting from about the age of eighteen months and even memorize numbers up to about ten, she won't understand the concept of numbers until she is about two and a half. Being able to count from memory will give her a head start in the coming months and years.

Introduces the idea of time

Counting while dad hides will demonstrate the concept of time to your child: the waiting comes to an end after a certain amount of time. When she is old enough to really get her head around waiting and time, she will be at an advantage if she's already had some exposure to the principles.

Helps understanding of sequencing

Learning to play hide-and-seek will teach your toddler about sequencing: that is, how events take place in a particular order.

Eases separation anxiety

Lots of toddlers go through a phase of clinging to mom and dad and becoming very anxious when they are out of sight. Clinginess peaks at around fifteen months and usually eases by the age of two. Playing hide-and-seek will show your toddler that it can actually be quite fun if mom or dad are hiding and out of sight. It will also give her a sense of control and empowerment over mom and dad's absence and so help to ease her anxiety.

95 Rough and Tumble

Rolling around on the floor with your child or having a gentle pillow fight can be great fun, and this is an activity where dad really comes into his own. Lifting your toddler high in the air, swinging him around or encouraging him to clamber all over you is the kind of play that comes very naturally to dads. From mom's point of view, these kinds of activities get toddlers very excited and worked up, so she may dread dad playing rough-and-tumble games at bedtime because children take a long time to get to sleep afterwards. A game of monsters or play-fighting will push stress hormones (adrenaline) up and it can take up to an hour for hormone levels to return to normal and for your child to be calm again.

Provided it's well before bedtime, rough-and-tumble games are a great way for toddlers to have fun with dad. In fact, they should be encouraged because there are so many benefits, and although it can look as though dad is being rough, children love this type of play. Boys are particularly keen on

What you need

- Floor space (ideally carpet or grass)
- Pillows

Benefits

Teaches self-control

Learning the 'time out' rule will teach your toddler to stop wrestling when he is being too rough. This will help to teach him to control himself when he's playing rough games.

Could provide protection against future bullies

Your toddler will learn that he has the power to call 'time out' or just 'no' when he's had enough and wants Dad to stop. This will teach him that his say is important and that

he has the power to get out of a situation he doesn't like. One day this could give him the self-confidence to stand up to bullies.

Expends energy

Rough-and-tumble games are very energetic and are a great way to wear your toddler out. Children need physical activity, and an exhilarating game of monsters is particularly good for releasing pent up energy and frustration.

play-fighting because exposure to androgen (a male hormone) in the womb affects foetal development and predisposes boys towards physical activity and rough and tumble. Because this type of behaviour tends to be more male than female, dads are more likely to engage in vigorous play with their sons than moms are.

The key with rough and tumble is learning when to stop. As your toddler approaches two and is able to speak, you can agree to call 'time out' or 'stop' when things are getting too rough. It's important that dad calls time out too as soon as play-fighting starts to turn a little aggressive. Eventually your child will learn the boundaries and this will be extremely useful when it comes to playing with other children.

Everybody's different

Some children enjoy rough and tumble more than others, so don't force your child to play if he doesn't want to. If little girls, or indeed their mothers, love rough and tumble, that's fine too. The only rules are that everyone should have fun and no one should get hurt.

96 Bags, Baskets and Pockets

As your toddler approaches her second birthday, she'll start to enjoy possessions and will have fun keeping small toys all to herself in pockets and bags. She'll suddenly hate sharing, especially with other children, and will guard favourite toys with increasing ferocity. This is a natural development stage, and possessiveness occurs as children become aware of their sense of self and want to define themselves as individual and separate.

Your toddler will really enjoy having pockets so that she can fill them with little treasures. As well as toys, you could give her a tissue to blow her nose on, a plaster in case she falls over or even a tiny photo of you and your partner. She will also enjoy having her own bag. You can buy children's rucksacks or pull-along suitcases, but she will probably be just as happy with a cloth or paper shopping bag or even an old handbag.

What you need

Any of the following:
- Toddler clothes with pockets
- Paper shopping bags
- Old handbags
- Small toys and other safe items
- Ride-on vehicle with trailer
- Toy buggy

Benefits

Improves dexterity
Getting small objects in and out of pockets and bags requires dexterity and will help further develop your toddler's fine motor skills.

Encourages planning
Packing a bag of toys to play with later (for example, in a doctor's waiting room) will encourage your toddler to think ahead and plan. If she's putting a favourite toy into a tractor or buggy at playgroup, she'll be planning and thinking about how to keep the toy all to herself and away from the other children.

Promotes sharing
As your toddler becomes more possessive, she'll start to learn about sharing as she tearfully watches a toy being given to another child when it is their turn. Although, developmentally, she's still too young to be able to share, your toddler will nonetheless become aware of the principles of sharing. Before children become possessive, the issue of sharing is unlikely to be raised so they are unaware of the concept.

She'll enjoy putting things in and taking them out of her bag, and pottering about at home clutching it and adding to her collection of possessions. She may place value on quite random objects: a broken computer mouse, an old mobile phone or a cheap plastic toy from a party. She'll choose certain objects and want to keep hold of them.

If you're going out, you could suggest that your child has her snack or packed lunch in her own bag. She'll love the idea of holding and possessing it. And if you're going to a restaurant or the doctor's, for instance, perhaps help your toddler to pack a few books and toys in her bag to keep her amused while she waits.

Another popular way to collect possessions at this age is to keep them in the back of a ride-on toy vehicle. If you're at a playgroup and there's a tractor with a trailer, your little one will love choosing a toy, putting it in the trailer and riding around knowing that it's 'her toy' and the other children can't play with it. Of course, you'll need to intervene at some stage and help her to share with the other children, but until someone else wants a turn let her relish her wonderful feeling of possessiveness. Likewise, she may also enjoy loading up a toy pram or buggy with a specially chosen toy.

97 Sticking Fun

Sticking is a quick and easy way to get creative and make a picture, and toddlers love it. Of course, you and your child can put your imaginations together to come up with any creation you like, but below are some ideas to get you started.

If you're not particularly creative, an abstract picture is ideal. At this age your toddler will have no expectations and will be happy with the process of gluing. She won't even be thinking about what she's going to make. Simply cover a table with newspaper, then give your child a piece of paper, a clean paintbrush, a dish of glue and some pictures cut out of magazines and show her how to stick the pictures onto the paper. The end result won't look impressive or creative, but your child will have great fun. For added variety you could give her some felt shapes to stick on the paper.

For something a little more creative, you could make a face. A paper plate makes an ideal canvas. Begin by showing your toddler how to stick on the eyes – she'll be particularly interested in these – and then help her to add some wool for hair and a felt nose and mouth; you could cut out these shapes in advance (a triangle for the nose and a rectangle for the mouth is sufficient if you want to keep things simple).

For something a bit different, your toddler could make a penguin. For the base layer you'll need a large black oval or penguin shape – fat at the bottom and narrower at the head. On to the fatter area stick a slightly smaller white circle to make the penguin's tummy. Your toddler can decorate the tummy with glitter glue. To make the eyes, cut out two white circles and draw two black pupils in the middle. Stick these on to the penguin's face, then stick on a small orange, oval nose. For the feet, cut out two orange semi-circles and cut three toes out of the flat side. Stick these on to the bottom of the penguin.

What you need

- Child-friendly glue
- Paintbrush
- Plain paper
- Magazines
- Glitter glue
- Felt shapes

To make a face:
- White paper plate
- Self-adhesive eyes (available from craft shops)
- Wool
- Red felt

To make a penguin:
- Black, white and orange paper

Glitter glue

As your toddler is bound to smear glue over much of her picture, we would recommend glitter glue rather than regular glue as it will look prettier.

Benefits

Improves dexterity

Spreading glue, picking up small shapes and arranging them on the paper require good hand–eye coordination and will develop your toddler's fine motor skills.

Introduces the concept of colour

Your toddler won't learn her colours before the age of two but, in the meantime, she can learn that colours have names, and start to understand what colour is. You can help by asking, 'Do you want to stick yellow hair or brown hair onto the plate face?' and you can talk about the penguin's feet being orange.

Promotes creativity

Making things with your toddler encourages creativity, and seeing her finished work will give her a sense of accomplishment.

Aids concentration

Sitting down to make something will focus your toddler's mind and encourage her to sit still. She may only want to sit for a few minutes, but that's fine at this age.

98 Car Wash

When you wash your car, your toddler will be a very willing assistant. As she's not yet two, she won't actually be very much help but there's plenty you can give her to do, nonetheless. For maximum safety, this should be done in a private front garden or drive behind a closed gate; however, if you are on a quiet road your toddler can help as long as she stays on the pavement side, is very closely supervised at all times and is kept within easy reach of an adult. Ensure that your toddler can see you because she'll want to watch and imitate.

Take a little time to kit out your toddler with the things that you use to wash the car – her own bucket, sponge and cloth – then talk her through what you are doing: dipping the sponge into the bucket and squeezing it out; likewise with the cloth. To protect her skin, avoid adding harsh soaps and cleaning chemicals to your toddler's water. Using plain water is fine, but for fun you could add some children's bubble bath so that she has a lovely bubbly mixture to do her cleaning with.

What you need

- Your usual car-washing kit
- Small bucket
- Clean cloth
- Sponge

Hosing down the car at the end can be great fun. Your toddler can help you hold the hose and, if the jet isn't too strong, you can let her have a go at holding it on her own. The final polishing stage generally takes a while, so your toddler may not have the patience to assist for the duration, but she'll certainly be curious for a few minutes. Once you've finished, if your child has a toy ride-on vehicle you could clean that together. She'll be particularly enthusiastic as it's her own 'car', especially if she has her own bucket, cloth and sponge, which will make the task seem very grown-up.

Car care

If you're concerned that your toddler may inadvertently scratch the paintwork on your car, suggest that she washes the wheels and number plates as she won't be able to damage these.

Benefits

Boosts upper-body strength

Lifting her bucket will work your toddler's arms and shoulders and build her upper-back muscles. Rubbing away with her sponge will also work her upper-body muscles.

Raises understanding of scale

Helping to wash a full-sized car, then washing a toddler-sized vehicle will help to teach your child about different sizes. She'll start to understand the concept of big and small, and begin to relate her own size to the big and the small car.

Boosts understanding of the world

Your child will learn that cleaning the car makes it shiny, but she will also see that after a couple of weeks of going out on the road the car becomes dirty again. You can explain that the dirt is from dust, oil and other cars.

Boosts concentration

Your child will learn about concentrating on the task until it is complete. Even if she wanders off in the middle because she becomes bored, she'll see that you continue until the job is finished.

99 Body Shape

Unroll some wallpaper and get your child to lie down on it, then draw around her with a marker pen. Cut out the body shape and then you can draw on clothes together and colour them in. Stick the finished figure on the wall with the feet at floor level so it's the same height as your child.

What you need

- Roll of spare wallpaper (or cheap lining paper)
- Marker pen
- Scissors
- Crayons

Benefits

Promotes self-control
Your child will have to lie still for about a minute while you draw round her. This will require her to focus and be very disciplined.

Teaches sense of scale
Because the figure is life size, your toddler will get an impression of how big she is.

Helps language development
This is a fun way for your child to learn the names of body parts and items of clothing.

TODDLER

100 Hands and Feet

Draw around your toddler's hands, then cut out the shapes and stick them onto card of a contrasting colour to make a greetings card for grandparents or other family members. Your toddler can sign the card with her own personal scribble. Your little one could make a batch of cards to send as 'Thank You' cards after her second birthday.

Rather than cutting out the shapes to make cards, your toddler could have fun drawing on a watch, bracelets and rings. You can also do this exercise with feet, drawing on shoes. Alternatively, you could paint your child's hands and feet directly so that she can make prints on paper herself.

Benefits

Introduces the concept of writing
When your toddler 'signs' her name, she'll start to become familiar with the concept of writing, as well as learning how to hold a pen.

Boosts understanding of the world
As you draw on watches and rings you can talk to your toddler about what these are, and perhaps let her try on yours.

What you need
- Paper (coloured works well)
- Coloured card (different to the paper)
- Pens or pencils

Development Time Line

All babies and children develop at different rates: for example, the normal age range for taking the first steps or saying the first word is anywhere between nine and eighteen months. This time line shows the capabilities of babies and toddlers up to the age of two and is designed to give you a rough idea of what might happen when. We stress that you shouldn't expect your child to follow this to the letter as **all children are different**. We have included it here as we hope it will be a useful aid to playing with your child.

Birth: *Likes looking at faces more than anything else. Finds black-and-white objects easier to see than coloured ones.*

Six weeks: *Starts to enjoy looking at bright, primary colours.*

Two months: *Is able to grasp objects purposefully and will start to reach out and bash things whether he is on his back or tummy. Starts kicking vigorously.*

Two weeks: *May be able to lift his head briefly when on his tummy.*

Five months: *Discovers his toes and starts to suck them. Can lift his head up when he is lying on his back.*

Three months: *Will learn to control her arms and begin to use a soft rattle. Is able to support her head well. Will look around the room when being carried. Will start to babble, making lots of coo, goo, da, ma and ka sounds.*

Seven months: *Can sit up. Can switch on lights and post letters (with help).*

Six months: *Can roll from back to front. Her vision improves, enabling her to play with more complex toys. Is able to grab moving objects.*

Four months: *Will discover her hands and start to play with them. Her head control is even better and she can lift her head and shoulders up if she is on her tummy. Can roll from front to back.*

Eight months: *Can sit unsupported and may bang the highchair tray. If he drops a toy, he will look for it.*

Nine months: *Starts to follow simple actions such as clapping and waving. May make animal noises such as 'mooo'. Puts things into boxes and takes them out again. Starts to explore things with his mouth. Develops the pincer grip: picking up tiny objects between thumb and forefinger.*

Fourteen months: *Average age to start walking (but this varies greatly). Starts to learn body parts.*

Eleven months: *Learns to throw. Imitates: for example, pretending to use a telephone.*

Ten months: *Releases his fingers to drop objects deliberately. Early developers may stand up.*

Fifteen months: *Can stack wooden blocks and use both hands competently.*

Twelve months: *Says his first word. Cruises around furniture, perhaps even taking his first steps. Makes a few marks on paper with a crayon. Can carry three objects at once, nestling one in the crook of his arm.*

Sixteen months: *Learns to point to things. Starts to play with toy people.*

Twenty months: *Can do simple puzzles. Copies tasks like sweeping. Can 'label' pictures: if you ask where the 'cat' is, he may point to the picture of the cat.*

Twenty-four months: *Undresses himself. Walks upstairs.*

Twenty-two months: *Becomes possessive of toys and starts to resent sharing. Loves keeping special toys in a pocket or bag.*

Eighteen months: *Can carry an object while walking. Fear sets in: may become afraid of dogs or vacuum cleaners. Can run quite quickly. Can scribble enthusiastically. Can sniff a smell such as a flower. Can drink through a straw. Will sing the words to songs.*

Resources

We have tried to keep the activities simple so that you don't need to buy too much. However, if you do want to shop for certain items, you may find the following websites helpful.

www.amazon.co.uk Baby equipment and toys; bells; craft supplies; glove puppets; music boxes; nursery-rhyme CDs; wind chimes; toys for toddlers; sandpits and supplies.

www.amazon.com Sensory brushes; see above.

www.elc.co.uk (Early Learning Centre) Dressing up; play dough; sand pits and supplies; toy gardening equipment; toys for babies and toddlers.

www.mamasandpapas.com Baby equipment and toys.

www.mothercare.com Baby equipment; dressing-up; toys for babies and toddlers.

www.photobox.co.uk Fridge-magnet photo frames.

www.toysrus.co.uk / www.toyrsrus.com Baby equipment; dressing-up; toys for babies and toddlers.

www.zazzle.com Fridge-magnet photo frames.

Index

Page numbers shown in **bold** refer to benefits.

achievement, sense of **139**
ambidexterity 164
animals: familiarity with 98–9
     introducing to 162–3
     love of **98**
     making sounds of 94–5
anticipation **73**, **77**
anxiety: relieving **113**, **140**

baby carriers: using 29
baby gym 36–7
baby walkers 51
back muscles: strengthening
     21
bags 192–3
baking cakes 136–7
balance **51**, **57**, **65**, **77**, **83**,
     85, **123**
balls: rolling 76–7
baskets 192–3
bath-time 32–3, 92–3, 144–5
bells: attaching to chair 28
body parts: learning **135**,
     142–3
body shape: drawing 198
bonding **13**, **19**, **29**, **33**, **57**,
     85, **147**
books 68–9, **69**
bouncing 50–1
bouncy chair: baby in 22–3
boxes: filling and emptying
     96–7
     play in 126–7
brain development: boosting

26, 30, 57
bread: making 140–1
brush therapy 78–9
bubble-blowing 114–15
building and knocking down
     104–5, 148
bullies: protection against **190**

café play 172–3
cakes: baking 136–7
     decorating 138–9
car washing 196–7
cause and effect **28**, **37**, **39**, **48**,
     73, **87**, **101**, **151**
chasing 159
city on the floor 120–1
clinging 63
cold symptoms: easing **23**
colic: relieving **21**, **43**
colours **139**, **151**, **195**
comfort: providing **167**
communication **13**, **41**
     talking to baby 18–19,
     146–7
concentration **75**, **124**, **151**,
     181, **195**, **197**
control, sense of **105**
conversations: first 46–7
     skills **75**
cooking 178–9
coordination **42**, **44**, **51**, **79**,
     98, **102**, **121**, **175**
     hand–eye **30**, **37**, **48**, **77**,
     148, **153**, **164**
copying parents 152–3
counting **145**, **189**
crawling 60, 77, 84–5

creativity **164**, **169**, **195**
cruising 116–17
crying: reducing **29**
curiosity: encouraging **89**

dancing 158
development: time-line 200–3
dexterity **70**, **73**, **87**, **89**, **97**,
     101, **135**, **136**, **139**, **149**,
     153, **155**, **157**, **163**, **179**,
     192, **195**
dimensions: learning about **69**
distractions **142**
drawing 164
dressing oneself **185**
dressing up 184–5
dribbling: reducing **136**, **169**
drinking straws 183
dropping objects 100–1

energy: expending **190**
enquiring mind **97**
entertainment **48**, **67**, **75**
exploring: motivating **117**
eyes 16
     strengthening muscles **17**,
     23, **26**

face to face 44–5
failure: coping with **85**
fear: coping with 63
feet: drawing 199
fitness **85**, **119**, **123**
flattened head syndrome:
     reducing **17**, **21**, **41**
focusing **13**
food: anxiety about **70**

food play 70–1
friendship: encouraging **98**
fun: promoting **81**, **87**
fussy eating: combating **179**

gingerbread figures 134–5

hand–eye coordination **30**,
     37, **48**, **77**, **148**, **153**, **164**
hands: drawing 199
     playing with 48–9
head control: developing **29**
healthy eating **125**, **133**, **140**
hearing 14–15
helping 82, 154–5, 160–1
hide-and-seek 188–9
hiding objects 88–9
humour, sense of 60, **102**,
     105, **115**

imagination: developing **133**,
     173, **175**, **185**
imaginative play **107**, **126**, **153**
independence **97**, **117**
interaction: promoting **35**
investigative skills **149**

Jack-in-the-box 72, **73**
judgement **159**

kicking about 38–9

language development **19**, **47**,
     55, **65**, **69**, **81**, **82**, **90**, **95**,
     97, 110–11, **126**, **135**, **142**,
     145, **147**, **165**, **167**, **181**,
     198

laughing 40
legs: exercises 34–5
    strengthening muscles **51**
library: pretend 170–1
lipstick art 168–9
listening: encouraging **53**, **95**

magnets 130–1
make-believe play 152–3
mathematical skills **101**, **115**,
    129, **148**, **149**, **155**, **161**
memory **15**, **35**, **65**, 124, **142**,
    151, **173**, **181**, **182**
messy play 111
mimicking **177**
mobile phones 107
mobiles 26–7
mood: uplifting **55**
motor skills **126**
movement **28**, **79**
moving objects: watching
    24–5
muscle control **115**
muscle development **17**, **21**,
    23, **26**, **33**, **35**, **41**, **51**, **65**,
    67, **133**
music 54–5, 86–7
musical ability **182**

nappy fun 40–1
nappy rash: easing **35**, **39**
nature: introduction to **91**,
    132–3, **163**
neck muscles: strengthening
    17, **21**, **41**, **51**
nesting 149
numerical skills **151**

object permanence **63**, 88
office: pretend 176–7
olfactory sense **167**
'other', concept of **44**
outdoor play 91, 132–3
outings 52–3, 80–1, 124–5

park play 122–3
pasta: threading 125
patience: teaching **186**
peekaboo 62–3, 74–5
photos 90, 130–1
physical activity **51**
planning **135**, **155**, **159**, **192**
play: benefits of 6–7
    in early weeks 10–11
    learning through 110–11
    time spent 10–11
    time to stop 11
playdough 156–7
playground politics **123**
playgrounds 122–3
pockets 192–3
pouring **173**
pretend play 106–7, 170–7
pulling faces 11, 12–13
puppets 74–5
push-along toys 118–19

rattles 42
reaction times **159**
reading 68–9
reassurance: providing **186**
reflux: easing **23**, **51**
relaxation **15**, **79**
responsibility: learning about
    163

rhythm, sense of **87**, **158**
roly-poly 66–7
rough and tumble 56–7,
    190–1
running 159

safety 67
sand play 112–13
scale, sense of **121**, **125**, **157**,
    197, **198**
school: preparing for **177**
scientific concepts **93**, **101**,
    105, **113**
scribbling 164
self-awareness **79**, **117**
self-control **98**, **171**, **190**, **198**
sensitivity: increasing **30**
sensory development **91**, **113**,
    133, **140**
separation anxiety 63, **189**
sequencing 63, **173**, **189**
setting the table 154–5
sharing **192**
shop play 174–5
singing 35, 64–5, 182
sitting up **77**
skills: teaching **107**
smell, sense of 166–7
smiling 11
social interaction **19**, **44**, **57**
socializing **53**
soothing **15**, **19**, **25**, **41**, **55**,
    113, **115**, **121**, **157**, **181**
sorting **161**
sounds: getting used to 14–15
    locating **15**, **89**
spatial awareness **135**

speech: development **136**,
    169, **183**, **186**
    muscle control for **115**
stacking 149
stamina: boosting **158**, **159**
standing 60
sticking fun 194–5
stimulation: providing **25**
story time 180–1
stranger-phobia 63, 111
swimming 53
swings 83

taking turns **171**
talking: to baby 18–19, 146–7
    development 110–11
team work **148**
teddy: looking after 186–7
throwing 102–3
tidying up 160–1
tiger up a tree 43
time: idea of **189**
tinfoil figures 165
tiredness: promoting **85**
    signs of 11
touch 30–1
towers: building 148
toys: action 72–3
trunk muscles: strengthening
    21
tummy play 20–1

understanding of world **23**,
    44, **53**, **75**, **81**, **82**, **90**, **136**,
    145, **147**, **161**, **165**, **167**,
    171, **173**, **175**, **197**, **199**
upper-body strength **197**

urine 33, 41

vestibular system **57**
vision: development **13**,
  16–17, **25**, 72
vocabulary 110–11, **115**

voice: recognition 18, **19**
  using **47**

walking 60, 116
  preparation for **39**, **117**,
  119

wash-day fun 150–1
watching: mother 22–3
  moving objects 24–5
water: confidence in **33**, **39**,
  53, **93**, **129**, **144**
  playing with 128–9

properties of **129**
weaning 70–1
weight transfer **67**
wind: relieving **21**
writing **175**, **177**, **199**

About the Authors

Simone Cave is a mother of three children and the co-author of several parenting books including *Your Baby Week by Week*, *Potty Training Boys* and *Potty Training Girls*. She was the Health Editor on the Daily Mirror for eight years and now works freelance, writing for national newspapers and magazines.

Dr Caroline Fertleman is Consultant Paediatrician at The Whittington Hospital, London, Honorary Senior Lecturer at University College London Medical School, and Consultant in Medical Education at the Institute of Child Health. She has co-authored several parenting books and is also a mother of three children.

Acknowledgements

We would like to thank Paul Johnson, Susan Leigh, Sunita Rao, Barbara Levy, Ian Jackson and Katie Golsby.

PICTURE CREDITS

Getty Images: Victoria Blackie 150; Vanessa Davies 121, 160, 179; Charles Gullung 132; Dan Kenyon 50; Gabrielle Revere 170

Istockphoto: Ana Abejon 191; Murat Aldemir 152; Naomi Bassitt 124; Blue Orange Studio 128; Stuart Bur 134, 135; Craftvision 176; Damir Cudic 8; Morgan David de Lossy 80; Steve Debenport 12; Lev Dolgatshjov 45; Jaimie Duplass 138; Fertnig 203; Flashon Studio 68; Shirly Friedman 127; Sergey Galushko 112; Stacey Gamez 183; Dorian Gray 159; Niko Guido 185; Oliver Hamalainen 141; Richard Hobson 64; Tom Horyn 108; Beth Jeppson 202; Krystian Kaczmarski 164; Milan Keser 172; Brad Killer 122; Paul Kline 40; James Knighten 24; Mikhail Kokhanchikov 32; Zoia Komisar 114; J Kullander 103; Emilia Kun 99; Isabelle Limbach 49, 62, 71; Marcus Lindström 29; Sean Locke 180, 196; Pavel Losevsky 46; Jason Lugo 18, 84; Julie Maerchant 58; Michael Mattner 66; Gary Martin 187; Nathan Maxfield 200; Michelle Milliman 86; Ekaterina Monakhova 162; Alex Motrenko 92; Laura Neal 74; Nyul 36; Onebluelight 91, 118, 166; Gergo Orban 146; Justin Paget 43; Youra Pechkin 20; Thomas Perkins 193; Viktor Pravdica 15; Ivelin Radkov 94; Nina Shannon 158; Leigh Schindler 137; Svetlana Shapiro 144; Igor Stepovik 27, 56; Jenny Swanson 14; Craig Swatton 203; James Tutor 188; Jo Unruh 38, 201; Jaroslaw Wojcik 76; Xabicasa 153; Nicole S. Young 83; Maria Zoroyan 157

Mother & Baby Picture Library: Ian Hooton 52, 104

Carl Golsby 100, 131 (top right), 149; Neilski 131 (below)

Specially commissioned photography by Emma Peios: 16, 22, 28, 31, 34, 42, 54, 78, 82, 88, 90, 96, 106, 116, 125, 143, 148, 154, 165, 168, 175, 182, 195, 198, 199

Eddison Sadd Editions would like to thank the models who attended the photoshoot for this book: Alaila, Archie, Bruce, Freddie, Grace, Gracie, Isobel and Jimmy.

EDDISON • SADD EDITIONS

Creative Director Nick Eddison
Mac Designer Brazzle Atkins
Editorial Director Ian Jackson
Senior Editor Katie Golsby
Proofreader Peter Kirkham
Indexer Dorothy Frame
Production Sarah Rooney